FULL THROTTLE

FROM THE BLUE ANGELS TO HOLLYWOOD STUNT PILOT

SCOTT "INTAKE" KARTVEDT

Say yes
Intake

HIGH PERFORMANCE
CLIMB

Cover Photo Credit: Erik Hilderbrandt

Cover art: Stacey Smekofske

Print ISBN: 979-8-9885460-1-6

DISCLAIMER

High Performance Climb is committed to publishing works of quality and integrity. In that spirit, we are proud to offer this book to our readers; however, the story, the experiences, and the words are the author's alone. Some individuals mentioned in the book may have different memories as they experienced this story from another point of view. The conversations in the book all come from the author's recollections, though they are not written to represent word-for-word transcripts. Rather, the author has retold them in a way that evokes the feeling and meaning of what was said, and in all instances, the essence of the dialogue is accurate.

Dedicated with eternal love and gratitude to Lisa,
and our boys Wyatt, and Nick.

ACKNOWLEDGMENTS

I have been exceptionally fortunate in my life because I say yes to opportunities, learn from mistakes and failures, and I am always willing to ask for help, advice, and knowledge, and this last element is critical.

I have never had an individual accomplishment. The stories you read in this book are the culmination of a tremendous support network, the result of others' belief in me and the opportunities provided to me and our family. I cannot recognize everyone who has helped, encouraged, and supported me. So, my apologies to anyone who reads this and feels unrecognized. Please know that hundreds, if not thousands, of people, have helped me during the pivotal moments of my life and journey.

Let's start at the beginning with my mom, Susan, and my dad, Maynard; my older brother Mikal (who inspired my competitive drive and is the self-proclaimed president of my fan club); and my sister Kristin who were instrumental during my foundational years. Since we were 15, Bobby Brust, my best friend, and our other high school friends, Billings, Brewer, Gilmore, Daluiso, Bush, Fasset, Cousins,

Spinazzola, and Viesel. My Pepperdine fraternity brothers and cross-country teammates.

The Navy list is long due to the exceptional impact serving our country had on our family. In no particular order, Admiral Tim "Timbo" Keating, Eric "Catfish" Brown, "JJ" Cummings, Kevin "Proton" McLaughlin "Turk" Green, Dan "Dino" Martin, Len "Loni" Anderson, Hunter "Hamster" Hobson, Kevin "Chickenbone" Colling, Dave "Wolfy" Silkey, Kieth "Judge" Hoskins, Scott "Banker" Ind, Jack "MILF" Becker, Matt "SHILOC" Morton, Dan "Stretch" Keck, Ed "Vanna" White, Pete "Gato" Catalano, Matt "Whiz" Buckley, Scott "Topper" Farr, Nicole "BADDOG!" Johnson, Pat "Blood" Driscoll, "Cello" Caceres, Bruce "Iron" Shank, Bruce "Doc" Winter, Andy "Woody" Lewis, John "JB" Allison, and Paul "Dorf" Olin.

All of the Sailors and Marines, past and present, of the US Navy Flight Demonstration Team, the Blue Angels. Every warrior of our combat squadron VFA-83, the Rampagers, the plank owners of VFA-101, the Grim Reapers, and the SSWFGD Sailors of my first fighter squadron VFA-192, the Golden Dragons.

My civilian transition guides Todd Oseth, Bryan Quigley, Mike McCasky, John "Snags" Weigand, and Rob Strickland. They helped me convert my warfighting skills to the corporate world and have been great mentors.

Randy "Howler" Howell for allowing lightning to strike twice in my life and flying with a group of professionals in a six-ship jet demonstration. To ALL my friends of the Patriot

Jet Team, the most exceptional, dedicated group of volunteers with whom I have worked.

The professionals I've worked with in the movie industry, Tom Cruise, Christopher "McQ" McQuarrie, Kevin "K2" LaRosa, Amy "Lovely" Byrne, Mary Boulding, Steve "Mothy" Moth, John Romain, and all of the other professionals in the industry.

My mentors and personal Board of Directors, Lisa, Bobby, Mikal, Kim "Sales" Woody, "Howler," Ron Looney, Dave "Hollywood" Anderson, Mike "Manny" Campbell, and Sergio "Serg" Galindo

And the wonderful people who helped bring my stories to these pages, Troy Lambert, Laura Einsetler, and the incredible photography of Erik "Erok" Hildebrandt and Krista Reyes

There are countless more, and I am humbled and grateful to all of them!

THE BEGINNING

On a warm spring day in San Diego in 1986, a group of my friends and I headed to the theater to see Top Gun, which had just come out. Ten or so of us, including my lifelong friend Bobby, went to our local theater and bought tickets and the typical movie snacks.

The movie started, and immediately the adrenaline started pumping. I felt an odd thrill as the theme music blared, and we watched the jets take off from the aircraft carrier. The movie had me hooked from the very beginning.

We watched as Maverick and Goose flew their F-14s against a couple of MiGs, creating the iconic moment of "inverted international relations." Then, despite his reputation for flaunting the rules (not to mention buzzing the tower and ticking off admirals), Maverick and his backseater, Goose, were sent to Top Gun -- the Navy's elite fighter school in Miramar.

We followed them through their training, cheering as they fought it out with one another and pushed each other to improve. We all adopted the now-famous line, "I feel the need...The need for speed!" As Maverick and Goose competed against other pilots and worked to improve their flying and teamwork, we became totally invested.

We watched in horror as Goose didn't survive punching out of their jet during a flat spin, something I didn't know anything about until then. Even though my parents were going through a divorce, I'd never lost a friend or colleague, a family member, or anyone else from my personal "unit." And I'd never flown in a fighter jet. None of us knew what the future had in store for us.

We all rooted for Tom Cruise's character to show up and graduate despite tragedy. We held our breath as Maverick finally took off, not knowing if he could overcome his grief over losing his friend and regain his flying prowess.

We all cheered when Maverick re-engaged the enemy in the final scenes and buzzed the tower to cheers from the crowd in the theater. At that moment, we were all part of something unique that we would never forget.

We'd never seen anything like it. Top Gun was the first movie to use actual planes and actual pilots instead of relying on computer-generated special effects, which were pretty bad at the time. This felt different. Real.

It didn't take long for us to see Top Gun again. And again and again. We were hooked. We dressed like the characters in the movie. Leather jackets, jeans, and t-shirts became our wardrobe of choice, topped with a pair of aviators.

Every time we watched it, we felt a little more of an adrenaline rush – the more we watched, the more I wanted to do what Maverick did. We must have seen it at least ten times.

We'd stand up and yell, dropping the famous line into our everyday conversations: "I feel the need...for speed!" We were already a close-knit group, but the shared interest in a movie brought us even closer together. It was as if we had stepped into Top Gun ourselves, and the experiences that crossed the screen became our experiences.

Those memories never faded. The movie showed us anything was possible, that hardship could be overcome, and that the bad guys could be defeated. Perhaps most importantly for me, it satisfied my need for an adrenaline rush. I grew up riding motorcycles and engaging in other activities that fed that need for something that got the endorphins flowing.

Living in California, often after seeing Top Gun, we'd drive up to Miramar to watch the F-14s take off one after another, their afterburners leaving a trail of flame behind them. The air literally shook, and the roar of their engines rumbled through our chests like thunder. Closer, the smell of jet fuel would have been thick, almost suffocating. The smell coated our tongues and almost numbed them. The air around the jets crackled and popped like a campfire, and as they accelerated and took off, the heat washed over us like a wave.

But I didn't know all of that then. I didn't know or understand how slick the carrier's deck was or how it would move under your feet as you run to your aircraft. I admired the planes from a distance, wondering what it would be like to fly one of them.

Top Gun resonated especially strongly with me since my grandpa had been a power plant chief in the Navy during World War Two, and my dad had attended the Naval Academy. The Navy was in my blood, and flying felt like my future.

That's what started it. Of all the guys in that group of friends, I am still in touch with, my friend Bob and I were the most serious about becoming fighter pilots.

After high school graduation, Bob went to San Diego State and joined the Air Force ROTC, determined to fly someday.

And me? I went to college at Pepperdine, majoring in accounting and figuring I would become a real-estate mogul.

I went to Pepperdine without ever having been to the campus before. I didn't realize it was affiliated with the Church of Christ. I chose that college because a friend from high school had an attractive older sister who attended there, and I thought, "Well if she went, there're probably other good-looking gals there."

I applied, and they accepted me. I drove a truck to class, and it was a little out of place among the luxury cars and new vehicles given to the students from wealthy families who were nothing like mine.

As I headed off to college, the situation in our family spiraled out of control, especially financially. My parents' divorce was still fresh, and my dad's law practice struggled as he tried to keep up with alimony and child support payments. He also helped me with tuition, but I could see that was not sustainable.

I knew I had to do something, so I got a job soon after I arrived on campus.

I scanned the school paper to find something I qualified for that would make me the most money. For me, that meant slinging food in the cafeteria. I was surrounded by wealthy, demanding people who didn't view me as an equal but instead as someone there to serve them. This powerful, eye-opening lesson about how people should not be treated would stay with me for the rest of my life.

Even then, I was pretty confident, and it didn't get under my skin. I just watched and learned, and when I turned 21, I left that job and started working at a local bar. I also waited tables in a place called the Malibu Omelet Parlor during my sophomore, junior, and senior years, right across from the main pier in downtown Malibu.

I started by studying general business, really took to accounting, and made that my major. I joined one of the local fraternities. I loved being a part of it and became their social activity chairman, and I ended up putting together dozens and dozens of parties throughout my college years.

I lived with three other guys in a condo right down the street from the school. For a group of students, it was a really wonderful house. I was the only one who worked since their parents supported my roommates. I managed about 30 hours a week between bartending and waiting tables while taking a full load.

Since they didn't have to work, they were a little bit more into the academic side of college, and I was a little bit more into the Malibu lifestyle and just studying when I could make the time. It was the same way I had approached high school, and I really didn't know any better; otherwise, my GPA might have been higher than it was.

But I've got a pretty large personality, and that was able to help me overcome my academic weaknesses.

When it came to those first college relationships, I fell in love during my freshman and the first part of my sophomore year. Her name was Laurie, the first woman I ever loved. But I went a little overboard in my desire to be with her. In the end, I probably just choked out that relationship because I wanted to spend so much time with her, and I was so enthralled.

In hindsight, I'm sure that a part of what drove that obsession was jealousy and the fact that I couldn't get enough of her. Unintentionally, I pushed her away, and I found myself heartbroken.

After that, I dated around a lot and got the reputation

that I would date a gal for a few weeks, and then I would move on to the next one.

But early in my time at Pepperdine, I met this young woman, Lisa King. I met her on a Pepperdine-sponsored ski trip to Steamboat Springs during my first year.

We introduced ourselves to one another, and I thought she was pretty cute. But I was seeing Laurie, and she was seeing someone else at that time, so an introduction was all that happened.

Then during our sophomore year, I went to a play put on by the theater department, and she was a part of the cast. She did a great job, and I remember thinking, "Wow, she has really nice legs."

Of course, I knew who she was. She knew who I was, but we did not know each other well at all.

Coincidentally, she went to Germany as an exchange student. I did, too but at a different time. In my junior year, I kept busy with the fraternity setting up ski trips, parties, and other activities. Mainly I just partied like all college kids, working toward the graduation finish line.

But I had more classes with Lisa that year. We were both business majors and started flirting and joking around in the back of classes. Unlike me, Lisa is an incredible academic and took copious notes during class.

I remember one particular class where we had a professor who literally read the material out of the book. He didn't do any lectures or add anything to the reading; on top of it, he had a dull, monotone voice.

I wasn't engaging and getting what I needed from the

class. While Lisa still took tons of notes, I read a Calvin and Hobbs book behind my textbook. She asked me why I wasn't paying attention, and I smiled.

"He's just reading from the textbook, and I can do that later," I told her.

"How do you study, then?"

"I study really intensely for short periods of time."

"So you cram for the exam," she said.

It's one of the times I remember joking around with her, but there were others in the classes we shared. We were both headed for graduation, and I thought she was a lot of fun to be in class with.

During our senior year, we worked on a team project together: Lisa, myself, and three other guys. We had to assemble a 250-page paper and present it, almost like a capstone project for our business degree. We all worked closely throughout the semester before finally completing and presenting the report.

We hit a home run on the presentation. I was bartending then, so we went to where I worked after class because I got half-price drinks there. We ended up drinking, partying, and having a really great time.

The other guys on that project were probably attracted to her too. Fortunately, I was a little hipper than they were, or I just had a more prominent personality. I ended up kissing her for the first time that night.

I didn't know what to say when I saw her the next day. So I asked her out to dinner. As you can probably tell by now, things went really well.

We ended up dating that whole summer. As I said, at that point, I had a reputation for not dating anybody for more than a week or two, but summer turned into fall, and I said, "Wow, I didn't think our dating would last this long."

"Yeah, I didn't either, based on your reputation," she answered.

"Well, I'm still having a great time."

"Me too," she said. And so we just kept dating as our lives moved beyond college and into what would become the rest of our lives.

2

RE-IGNIGHTING THE DREAM

What Did I Learn in College?

I probably partied way too much. I was an average student, right at a 3.0 GPA. But I got to know several people I worked with in the business department. And I was not afraid to ask for help when I needed it, which would pay off for me in a big way later. And I had a good friend in the accounting department named Sam Grable, who also had a large personality. We had a really good time together. And, of course, I met Lisa.

But when college was over, I needed a job. So I went to work for Kleinfeld Peat Marwick Gordimer (KPMG), an international accounting firm, and started to put my degree to use. But almost as soon as I started that job, I got a call from who else but my high-school friend Bob, one of the guys I'd gone to Top Gun with. The one who said he wanted to fly jets, too.

He'd finished his ROTC training and graduated college, and he called with some news.

"I'm doing it," he said. "I've selected jets, and I'm going to fly jets with the Air Force."

That reminded me of watching Top Gun repeatedly in the theater, dreaming of flying jets off carriers. Bob wouldn't be flying off carriers in the Air Force, but he would be flying fighter jets.

So I responded the only way I knew how. "Well, then I'm going to do it, too."

Of course, I had no idea how to do that, but I figured I could figure it out. So I pulled out the Yellow Pages, found the number for the Navy Recruiters in L.A., and got the number for the Los Angeles recruiting depot. I called them up and said, "I want to be a pilot."

"Okay, we'll pass you through the aviation people," they said.

They put me on hold, and a gentleman named Lieutenant Novansito answered the phone.

"My name is Scott Kartvedt, and I want to fly airplanes off of ships," I told him.

"So does everybody," he said, probably silently cursing Tom Cruise and the Top Gun craze that hadn't died out yet, even more than four years later.

"Yeah, but I think I can do it," I said.

So he invited me to come down to complete some paperwork and take some tests.

I'll never forget heading to the recruiting office. I went

down to the L.A. recruiting depot with all the young men and women who had GEDs and were trying to enlist in the Navy. I had transitioned to work for KPMG as an accountant fresh out of college and was used to a much more professional interview type. When I walked in, I was wearing a suit and tie, prepared to sit down with someone and answer a lot of questions.

I walked into a room full of kids sitting in plastic chairs, attempting to fill out what I felt was pretty basic paperwork.

"All right. Put your last name first and then your first name," the recruiter told them. He'd walk around the room from row to row, and I'd hear him say, "No, your last name goes first. Then your first. No, no, your last name. And then put the city and state."

"How do you spell California?" one recruit asked.

I couldn't believe it. "Oh my god," I muttered to myself.

There was one kid that was so far behind. I just pulled him next to me. "Stop asking questions. I'll help you fill out your form. You'll be just fine," I told him.

Helping others in various stages of their careers strangely foreshadowed many things I would do later in my Navy career, but in the fall of 1989, this was just the beginning.

So I applied for an aviation slot and took all the required tests and physicals. But the Navy doesn't make decisions like that quickly, and a year later, I got the call that the board had met and selected me to enter training.

That was January 1991. When I got the call, Desert Storm was playing out on the television news, and I wondered what

I had done. Lisa and I were still dating, and she knew I had applied and this was my dream.

I was ready to go and serve no matter what else was happening in the world. Flying for the Navy was the dream, but much more work awaited me. The timeline for becoming a pilot, even just the training, takes a lot of time.

For me, it looked like this:

- First, I started by attending Aviation Officer Candidate School (AOCS) in Pensacola, Florida. I graduated from that training in November of 1991.
- Immediately I headed for Primary Flight School on December 9th of that same year.
- In June, I selected jets, the first step in my journey to flying fighters.

Now, in 1993 and 1994, getting to fly the plane you wanted was pretty competitive. Unless you were the top in your class, the Navy would choose for you based on their needs. Initially, I wanted to fly A-6s because I thought it would be just an incredible platform to fly, and many A6 pilots were transitioning to F/A-18s anyway. I really thought that is what I would end up flying.

I was number two in my class, right behind Hunter Ellis, who some of you may know was prominent in the reality show, Survivor back in the day.

That meant we could both select the team we wanted to

join and so out of that, I ended up heading to the F/A-18 Training Unit in Jacksonville.

From there, my life was about to take another pretty incredible turn.

3

THE I-10 HONEYMOON AND TAKING OFF

As a brief aside, let me explain the events that led up to Lisa and my wedding, which happened right between my selection of jets and entering advanced fighter training in Kingsville, Texas.

For Christmas in 1991, just after I graduated in Pensacola, Lisa gave me a massive painting of the Blue Angels in flight over Point Lobos, California. She signed the back, "Always Pursue your Dreams," in giant letters, strangely predictive of what would come later.

As I made my way through flight training in March of 1992, I found out Lisa was moving from one apartment to another in L.A., and I decided that would be an excellent opportunity to ask her to marry me. So I flew out to California to help her move.

I planned to pop the question up at Lake Arrowhead. We went up, and I deliberately picked a fight with her the night

17

before at dinner with our parents to throw her off the idea that we might get engaged that weekend.

I pulled her dad aside after dinner. Lisa's mother had passed away in 1989, and when I told her dad I wanted to marry her, he promised to give me her mother's wedding ring for her to wear, so I thought I would have it to give to her that weekend.

"Hey," I said as we went outside. "I'm going to ask your daughter to marry me in the morning."

"Ah, that's great!" he said. He didn't mention the ring or say anything like, "Oh, yeah, I've got that right here." So the next day, I had nothing to offer her except a proposal.

The following day, I took her to breakfast, and we had waffles if I recall correctly. We walked along the lake, and she walked ahead of me a little way and sat down on a rock. It was early spring, so we had the beach pretty much to ourselves.

Gosh, I really want to marry this girl, I thought. But this is a big commitment. Come on, God, show me a sign.

In the distance, church bells rang, and two F-4s from March Air Force Base flew over. I figured that was pretty definitive, no matter what you believe.

So I walked over and got down on one knee, no ring, just my heart in my hand, so to speak, and asked her to marry me. Needless to say, she said yes.

At the time, Lisa was the event coordinator for Pepperdine School of Business, so she could organize a party quickly. By the time I got back to work at the end of the next week, the entire wedding was planned.

I completed my primary flight training in Pensacola and was ordered to report to my intermediate and advanced jet training in Kingsville, Texas, on July 3, 1992.

So I gathered my stuff, left Florida, headed out on a fourteen-hour drive to Texas, and dropped everything off at a storage unit there. Then I headed to California, arriving just in time for Lisa and me to get married.

It was a beautiful ceremony, and a lot of people came out to support her, in part because her mom had passed away. There had to be at least 350 people there. The wedding took place at the San Bernardino Presbyterian Church, where she went growing up. Then the reception happened at the National Orange Show, a large conference venue.

Then we rented a U-Haul, grabbed her stuff, and headed for Kingsville, all in a period of days, with no time for a honeymoon or even a side trip. For anyone who has ever driven from California or anywhere west to east or even east to west through Texas, you know how long it takes to get through that state. So we joke that we had the I-10 honeymoon because we spent so much time on that road that week.

The beauty was that Lisa understood and supported my commitment, even at this early stage in my military career. We'd just gotten married and moved to a new place halfway across the country, and she didn't hesitate. And that would be far from our last move. In fact, it would be the first of many.

We were only in Kingsville until March 11 of 1994. Then we moved again to Jacksonville, Florida, for F/A-18 training.

As soon as I completed that, we moved to Japan in 1995. We were now an international couple. But when I say that, you have to understand that I still did the usual military stuff: I deployed on a carrier for weeks or months at a time, and Lisa made our home in a completely different country.

And that's where our first son was born. It's a pretty wild story because I was out on the USS Independence during the final trimester of her pregnancy.

We had pulled into port in Australia for a break. A friend we flew with in Japan who was flying F/A-18s in Australia on an exchange from the United States was living in Newcastle, about an hour north of Sydney. Four of us drove up to his house to stay for a couple of days and essentially partied with him while we were in port, playing some golf and having a good time. I happened to be on a golf course with a few guys, Andy "Woody" Lewis, Mike "Beef" Wellington, and Dan "Hondo" Henderson.

Our friend Eric "Catfish" Brown stayed behind at Hondo's townhouse. There were kangaroos on the golf course, and we laughed and had a great time. Suddenly, a course Marshall drives up in a golf cart. And he says, "Hey, one of your wives is in labor."

Well, Woody had four kids and already had a vasectomy. Beef was divorced and didn't have a girlfriend. Hondo didn't have a girlfriend, which left me by default. That's how I found out that Lisa was in labor.

Woody and I jumped in a golf cart, returned to Hondo's, and packed everything up. He drove me to the airport about an hour south. And because he had four kids already, we were talking about being dads on the way there. I was excited out of my mind, and the squadron command knew I would start leave as soon as Lisa went into labor since we weren't at war. So I had the opportunity to do that.

Should you ever wonder who would pay those exorbitant, last-minute international airfares, that would be me. I walked into the Sydney airport, looked up on the board for the next flight, went over to the counter, and said, "I need a ticket on this upcoming flight to Narita. My wife's in labor."

It was something like eighteen hundred bucks one way in 1997.

As I boarded, all the flight attendants knew why I was flying. They were super happy for me. So when I landed in Narita, they rushed me through security with the crew. I jumped on a train and got home.

From when I was on a golf course in Sydney to when I was at Lisa's side in labor and delivery was less than 24 hours.

But it ended up being about five days before Wyatt was born. She had Braxton Hicks contractions, so we were waiting for her to go into labor and doing various things to pass the time.

We were at a movie, and Lisa wasn't sure whether her water had broken or if there was just some leakage, which is a little more normal. So we left the movie and headed for the emergency room like you do when you're nine months pregnant and think labor may actually be starting.

When we arrived, the doctors tested the fluid and determined Lisa's water had indeed broken. She wasn't quite dilated enough to give birth yet, so we were playing the waiting game. But then Wyatt started to show distress, which meant he was at risk. As a result, they decided to do an emergency C-section.

By this time, it was early in the morning of April 5, 1997.

The doctors asked her several questions before they started the surgery, and when they got to a common one, they got an unusual answer.

"How old are you?" one doctor asked.

"What time is it?" Lisa asked.

The doctor looked at me as if to ask, "What's wrong with her?"

"Well, since it's 1:20 a.m., she's 29. If you had asked her at 11:59, she would have been 28. Today's her birthday."

The surgery went well, obviously, and that meant Lisa and Wyatt would share the same birthday. And the bill for his birth at that hospital? Twelve bucks. So we still tease Wyatt that he was pretty cheap to bring into the world.

In typical military career fashion, I had 30 days at home before I had to return to the ship to meet my carrier qualification requirements. While I was in Japan with Lisa, the carrier had moved on to Singapore. So I flew there and joined the crew, and we eventually returned to Japan.

In November of 1997, seven months later, we left Japan and headed for El Toro Marine Corps Air Station, where I would serve as a Landing Signal Officer (LSO). We were only there for a year because the Navy was shutting that base down, and after that, we moved to Marine Corps Air Station Miramar, the former site of the Top Gun school. By that time, that naval aviation school had moved to Fallon, Nevada.

But the irony was not lost on me.

There I was, a successful aviator in my aircraft, living the dream Bob and I had so long ago. And yet, even then, my career was just getting started.

Because I knew there was something more I wanted. My next step was to apply to become a Blue Angel.

It wouldn't be easy, but it was my path to living my dream.

4

TAKE OFFS AND LANDINGS

It's worth mentioning here that a Navy career, or any other one for that matter, is much like the takeoffs and landings an aviator does on an aircraft carrier.

People often ask me which is harder on a carrier, landing or taking off. The truth of the matter is that answer is not as simple as it would seem.

Because you train to both. The catapult is intense when you first get launched. You're pushed back into your seat with those initial G-forces, and it all happens really fast.

You also train for the landings, and that is intense in its own way. It takes precise skill, practiced over and over, to hook the wire, which then slows you to a stop rapidly and immediately, throwing you forward against your restraints rather than back. But that moment, too, is over rather quickly.

The difference really comes down to control. When you take off from a carrier, you don't touch the controls. Essentially, you bring the throttles up, set the trim, salute, indicating you are ready to take off, and then take your hands off the controls.

I often describe the situation when you leave the ship this way: you are unsure whether you are a plane or a refrigerator. You're in the air, but you don't know whether you're flying yet or not. Since you leave the ship and go out over an open ocean, your frame of reference is suddenly gone. You know if you have your end speed and must trust that you do. So it can feel like you are rotating or even going down. Your body wants to fight that, and your reaction is often to push forward and fight that.

This is especially tough at night. I often describe it as being shot off the ship and into the inside of a basketball. The ship itself has some light, but they keep it dark at night for obvious reasons. As you take off, you lose that ambient light, and a pilot can become quickly disoriented.

This instinct to level out or push downward can even cause a pilot to go down. So when you take off in an F/A-18, you actually hang on to these two handles called "towel bars" until you're airborne, and you develop a feel for when you can take the controls.

We even had a couple of friends of mine in an F-14 Tomcat eject because they leveled off and didn't climb. Rico, the backseater, pulled the handles, and they splashed the plane. Of course, the ship stopped, and they launched the helicopters to go pick up the pilots.

We were on the Landing Signal Officer (LSO) platform, and I remember running to the ship's side and looking over. About sixty feet below, I could see Rico, all of his rescue stuff inflated, bobbing by on the flow.

I talked to him afterward, and of course, he described the moment of hitting the water, everything inflated, and being totally out of control. He looked up to see 400,000 tons of diplomacy coming at him at 30 knots (slowing down, of course), but the flow of the water around the ship directed him down the right side and past it.

But he had no idea that would happen. It felt like he would be run over at any second.

And career takeoffs, including my decision to apply for a spot with the Blue Angels, can be a lot like that. I felt I was qualified, I wanted to launch, but there were a lot of things out of my control. There were interviews to go through and an entire process to face. It was time to "rush the Blues."

I had to trust that those who made those decisions would see that I had the skills needed and the determination and dedication to become a valuable part of the team.

But landings are different. The landing is easier for pilots, not because they are physically easier, but because they are mentally easier. Pilots like to be in control, and you make all the calls on a landing. You can wave off if something is wrong and go back around. You're interacting with every-thing that needs to be done, and it is dependent upon your skill, not a cat shot or anyone else.

And I would learn quickly, through the application

process and as I moved forward in my career, that this analogy was true in so many different ways.

But at this time in my life, I faced a true test of that determination and dedication: the application process for the world's most elite aerial demonstration team.

5

BLUE ANGELS AND SQUADRON BIRTHS

In 1998, when we were living in El Toro, I first applied to join the Blue Angels flight team. I was just 30 years old.

When you interview, you enter a room where the sixteen officers sit around a table. Each takes a turn asking you questions or following up after you answer. But Doug "V8" Verissimo asked one that took me by surprise.

"Tell me about a time you made a mistake in an airplane," he said, leaning forward in his chair.

I told a story, but my cheeks grew red as I finished. It was a pretty dumb one, but I didn't want to make myself look like a bad pilot. Not that I had never made a mistake in an airplane, but I certainly didn't want to share them.

"That's it?" Verissimo said, raising an eyebrow. "That's the dumbest thing you've ever done in an airplane?"

I almost laughed because I knew it was a lame story. "Yes, sir, that's it," I said. I felt relieved.

But I didn't get selected that year. I would later find out why. By then, we had moved to San Diego and lived on base at Miramar in San Diego.

In fact, several naval aviators' wives were expecting at that time, including the spouses of instructors and students. One of those couples was our terrific friends, Terry and Tracy Reynolds. We were kind of tracking along with the pregnancies, and then Lisa went into labor. I was at the squadron, and I got called out. We rushed to Balboa Naval Hospital.

We left Wyatt, who was almost two years old, with Terry and Tracy. Lisa had a long, drawn-out labor that ended in a C-section in the early morning of January 7, 1999.

Since I was in the hospital with her while she recovered from surgery, Tracy and Terry were watching Wyatt. As I was walking down the hall, I ran into Terry.

"Hey, Intake! How's Lisa?

"She's good," I said. "What are you doing here?"

"Oh, Tracy just had our baby," he said. "I just came from her room."

I stopped short. "Congratulations. But out of morbid curiosity. Where's Wyatt?"

"Oh yeah! He's with Tracy's mom and dad."

That ended a short-lived but heart-stopping moment.

During that two- or three-day period in the hospital, six F/A-18 pilots from the same squadron, VFMAT-101, either instructors or students, were all in the labor and delivery area with their wives. We have a picture with all the dads and the babies. One of them was "Iguana" Agulera.

But unfortunately, tragedy would strike our group not long after that.

While at Miramar, I got more flight time and taught others how to fly F/A-18s. I took people out to the aircraft carrier for the first time, day and night, and trained them on low-altitude flight and other tactics. It was really a lot of flight time, around 400 hours a year.

And when the application period for the Blues came around, I applied again, even though I didn't make it the first time.

"Well, I'm going to go all in on this, kind of how I do most things," I thought. "Because I don't ever want to think that I only sort of tried. I want to say I did my very best, and if I was selected or promoted, or whatever it was, I could say I truly gave it my all."

Fortunately, I had a good friend on the team, Dave Silkey. His callsign is Wolfy.

"Here's the point of the interview," he told me. "You just have to tell the truth. The Blue Angels accept that we make mistakes, but they want to see that we're ready to admit them and willing to learn from them moving forward."

I followed all of Wolfy's advice. Again, The team selected me as a finalist, and I returned to the table to be interviewed again.

And it was Doug Verissimo who again asked, "Tell me about the dumbest thing you've ever done on an airplane."

And I said, "Okay."

Just tell them the truth, I thought.

So this is the story that I told him.

We were doing an air power demonstration off the coast of Japan. The Japanese CNO was visiting the Admiral of the carrier strike group on the USS Independence. Several other high-ranking naval officers from the Japanese Defense Force were also on board. At the time, I flew as a wingman with a department head.

One of the department heads, LCDR John "Pags" Paganelli, led our section of F/A-18s for this portion of the demonstration, which was to fly alongside the ship and drop our bombs to make a wall of water.

"Pags" would count down "three, two, one." Then we would deploy four five hundred pound bombs each. When they explode, a wall of water is created, and it sprays upward spectacularly.

To maintain safety, you have to be a certain distance, between half a mile and a mile from the aircraft carrier, so the ship and those watching are clearly out of the fragmentation pattern of the bombs.

No problem.

The department head was brand new to Japan but not new to flying. He was the flight leader for the exercise, and I was his wingman. I've always had good situational awareness, and I remember thinking that our altitude was a little low and that we were a bit too close to the carrier for this particular drop. Other aircraft were flying around performing various maneuvers for the demonstration, but once our approach was cleared, we entered the airspace inbound to the carrier.

As' we came in, I realized our angle towards the ship would put us inside the boundary for safety.

And I didn't say anything. Instead, I simply followed his lead. The ship was on my right side, and I was looking to the left. I'm waiting for his three, two, one pickle call to drop the bombs, and I am counting on him to be aware of how close we are and make the right safety call.

As it turned out, we were inside the fragmentation pattern. So when we dropped, the fragments from the bombs ended up strafing the deck of the carrier, including the crowd. That included the Japanese CNO. who dived behind Rear Admiral William "Willy" Moore Jr. No one was injured, thank God, but a bomb fragment went through the wing of a C-2 Greyhound aircraft sitting on the deck. It was a big, big deal.

The admiral was pissed and wanted to bring us up on attempted murder charges. The incident could have been much worse for my career than it was.

But the worst was we didn't know any of this until we landed when the demonstration ended. An extensive investigation followed, and investigators asked questions about what went wrong and how something like that could happen. There were two points to that investigation.

One, I was telling the truth, the way that I saw it, and based on my situational awareness, I wasn't trying to dime out the flight lead or make it seem like everything was his fault. I told them how things happened from my perspective.

I also acknowledged that this, at least in part, was my failure. I didn't advocate for safety, so my leadership effectiveness was impotent in that situation. Essentially, I put too much trust in his competency and not enough faith in my own experiencebn . It wasn't about whether my perception was correct or his understanding was wrong. But we should have at least talked about it in the interest of safety.

I finished telling that story to those assembled. Then I said, "I learned that even though I'm a wingman, I have as much responsibility for that flight as anybody else. And I need to be an advocate for safety. I need the courage to speak up because people could have been seriously hurt or even killed.

I remember Wolfy saying, "That was you?" Because the incident was very well-known in the F/A-18 community.

"Yes, it was," I said.

The amazing lesson I learned from my application with the Blues is that I was trying to tell them what they wanted to hear in year one. I was trying to say, "I don't make mistakes, and I can be as good as you guys."

That's not what they wanted to hear at all. They wanted me to own up and take responsibility and accountability for the failures, errors, and mistakes that I'd made and show that I could overcome them. Because if you can self-identify, then you can self-correct.

So I went from telling them nothing to telling them everything. And that was the year that I got invited to be on the team. But before that happened, they had another question for me.

"Scott," one of them asked. "Would you be willing to apply a third time? If you're not selected?"

And still, to this day, I think it was one of my best interview answers ever.

I said, "That is truly an unanswerable question. Because if I say yes, then you can pick someone else over me. If I say no, I appear unmotivated." I reiterated that my goal was to be selected for the 2000 team. It turned out to be the perfect answer.

And the takeaway was that we're all human, and human beings make mistakes.

But the human being that can acknowledge their error, learn from it, and move on, has unlimited potential.

And I was just about to find out what that potential truly was.

6

SAFETY AND DANGER CLOSE

While I waited to learn if the Blue Angels would select me or not, I decided to take a course to pad my resume because I wanted to add some safety qualifications to the rest of my skills. So I applied to The Navy's aviation investigation and safety school in Monterey, California. It was a six-week course, and I graduated in May of 1999 as a safety officer and a qualified accident investigator.

Just one month later, in June of 1999, the Marines of VMFAT-101 had an accident near MCAS Yuma, where I was an instructor. A student and an instructor crashed when their plane went out of control during a dog fight. They were in what is called a falling leaf maneuver, and the instructor, Capt. John "JP" Hesford, ejected successfully from their F/A-18. Unfortunately, the student, Capt. Douglas "Iguana" Aguilera, who we called "Iggy" and one of the new dads in the photo in the maternity ward, could not eject and lost his life.

As the most recently certified accident investigator in our squadron, the commander tasked me with conducting the inquiry to determine precisely what happened. The emotional challenge was that I had known the student, his wife, and his family. But I had to be objective.

As we looked into the series of events that led to the crash, we discovered there had been a failure in the ejection seat sequence. Typically, no matter who pulls the handle, both seats activate simultaneously.

We know things worked in the back seat, but it appeared that the sequence didn't fire correctly into the front seat.

The question that remained was. "Why didn't Iggy pull the handle himself when he didn't eject?" But the procedure then was to grab onto part of the canopy. We thought perhaps when the canopy was ejected, he was holding on to it while he remained strapped in, which essentially disabled his arms.

The crash occurred over the desert near Yuma, Arizona. Like any aviation accident scene, especially when you know the person who went down, it impacted everyone who had flown with him. Once we had finished the investigation, the work became a clean-up, not a salvage and recovery effort. The investigation team left the scene and went to write up the report.

But I had flown an F/A-18 down to Yuma, and as I departed, I wanted to fly out over the crash site to do a missing man flyover to say goodbye to Iggy. Even though he was a student and I was an instructor, we were also friends. Our wives had given birth at nearly the same time, and we had children the same age. He'd left that young child and his wife behind. So I took the jet and flew out from Yuma, descending pretty low and pretty fast. Over the impact crater, I pitched up, a single airplane missing man, and went vertical.

The investigators on the ground said it was really unbelievable because as I did that, the air behind me created a cyclone that originated in the crater and followed me vertically upward as I departed.

That was in June. In July, I got notified that I had been selected to join the Blue Angels. In some ways, it was a bittersweet moment. We'd just lost a pilot, completed an investigation, and I would be moving on to something new and exciting.

But like many other things I experienced in the military, I moved on to what was next for me. I reported to the Blue Angels in Pensacola, Florida, in September. Three pilots had been selected: myself, Major Hunter Hobson, a Marine, and Lt. Kevin "Chicken Bone" Colling.

When you first join the team, everyone calls you a khaki newbie because you wear khakis rather than the blue flight suit. And you follow the team around, travel with them, and listen and learn. Essentially, you're being indoctrinated into the culture of excellence surrounding the Blue Angels.

You wear those khakis right up until the last show of the season. Once that show is over, the current pilots and team members who are leaving don't wear their blue suits ever again. And the khaki newbies put their Blue Suits on.

Although sometimes you do put on a flight suit before you take over for those who are leaving. That's because when you first join the team, they are often on the west coast swing, a three-week tour that includes Fleet Week in San Francisco. Because of that, they take extra jets, and the newbies often help fly those to various show locations.

Anyway, we joined the team in September. On October 27, the team had a position meeting to determine who would fly in what position for the next season. Major Hobson, "Hamster," was a shoo-in for the number two position because that typically went to Marines. Kevin "Chicken Bone" Collings would fly number 3, and so was designated as 33 for the remainder of the 1999 season. I would be the number 7 pilot, referred to as 77.

The morning of the 28th, in Valdosta, Georgia, "Chicken Bone," the new number 33, was going to fly with the current number 3, Lt. Commander Kieron "Tater" O'Connor, to learn the ropes of being the left wingman, the first time he had flown in a show. I remember him running past me in the blue suit, ready to get in the back seat. The excitement radiated from his face. That's the last image I have of him.

During the circle-and-arrival maneuver, the diamond took off, planes one through four. They confirm their checkpoints and run their show lines. But that morning, "Tater," the number 3 pilot and Kevin "Chicken Bone" Colling, crashed their F/A-18 during those maneuvers, and both were killed.

I was on the ground, learning the role of narrator and shadowing Keith "Judge" Hoskins, who was the current number seven.

The incident hit all of us hard, and it was a national tragedy, immediately on the news all around the country and likely the world. "Blue Angel Jet Crashes, Two Pilots Killed." The headlines read.

A word here about military wives and the things they go through. I'd called my wife the night before and told her I'd been selected as the number seventy-seven and would be Blue Angel #7 the following season, but I hadn't really had time to fill her in on what that meant.

And the number three jet, which crashed, had the number 7 on the side because that was the 2-seat plane they were in that day.

So when the news reported the incident, they said the number 7 jet crashed with fatalities, and since the F/A-18 was a two-seater, Lisa assumed I had been killed.

After the news hit, she'd gathered with all the other wives in Pensacola, Florida, where the team was based. Cell phones were not as prevalent then as they are now, and even if they had been, the standard emergency response was to secure all cell phones to control the messaging around the incident.

As soon as possible, Doug "V-8" Verissimo, the current number five on the team and the one who had asked me the tough questions at my interview, jumped into a jet and flew to Pensacola. He had the terrible job of telling the wives gathered there whose family members would not be coming home.

It wasn't until that moment that Lisa knew I was okay. It wasn't the last time she would have to wait to learn if I was okay or not from someone else, but it was one of the first. Such moments are all too frequent for the spouses of naval aviators, who are true heroes for the stress and worry they endure.

But the ordeal wasn't over for us yet. The team gathered, and we mourned, and most of the team headed home.

But Boss Driscoll called me into his room because I had just qualified as an F/A-18 accident investigator and had recent experience working on the crash just a few months before.

"Intake," he said. "We need you to lead the investigation into this incident."

At first, I told him no. "I just finished one not long ago," I told him. "And it was exhausting. It's still fresh."

"I know it's tough," he said. "But you are our guy. We need you on this."

The other accident had been devastating on so many levels, and I was brand new, having only been a Blue Angel for a month.

But I knew my duty, and so I told him yes, I would do it.

And I called my wife that night, emotionally exhausted and sobbing because I knew just how challenging the following days and weeks would be.

So while other pilots and members of the team headed back home, I stayed with a group of enlisted personnel and a few others to go clean up the forest and find what we thought might be causal, essentially picking up airplane and human parts from the debris field, cataloging and collecting them, and analyzing the situation.

The air wing sent out a Navy captain, an O-6, to be the senior member of the investigation team. That wasn't unexpected because of the national interest in the incident and the news headlines, but I could not have anticipated what happened next.

7

MEMORIAL(S)

O ne of the most challenging things any pilot will have to do is to say goodbye to a teammate, friend, and colleague, let alone two of them. Other members of the Blue Angels planned the memorials for Kevin and Kieron while our investigation moved forward.

The memorials were scheduled, and those of us doing the investigation intended to go.

"Hey, Captain," I told the naval officer in charge, "we're going to shut down for a couple of days and go to the memorial service."

"Oh, no Intake. We don't have time for that," he told me. "I mean, we have a lot of work to do out here."

"Yeah, Captain, that's not going to work. Nothing that we do out here is going to prevent what happened or change it. But not allowing us to go home and mourn with our families

45

and teammates will have a lasting negative impact on us. We have to allow the team to mourn together."

He looked at me and blinked, almost like, "Who are you as a young lieutenant to tell me what's going to happen."

But I just started back and then restated, "We're going to go home. And we'll be back in four days."

"Okay," he said. And that's what we did.

So on November 3rd, we were in Pensacola, Florida. We had just buried Lt. Cmdr. Kieron O'Connor. The next day, we flew Fat Albert up to Virginia Beach for Kevin Collings's memorial service in Virginia Beach.

After the memorial, we were at a bar because the Navy and fighter pilots, warriors, if you will, generally celebrate the loss of the comrade through good cheer and celebration. So we were at a bar telling stories, letting off all of this emotion in grieving and mourning the way I think warriors have throughout time.

And I remember being pretty intoxicated when I got a phone call from my sister telling me that my mother had been diagnosed with cancer. This was only six days after the accident.

So I got up the following day, went to Arlington, buried Kevin, and then flew home to Pensacola. I picked up Lisa and the boys and flew to Las Vegas, where my mother lived.

When we arrived, they said she had a glioblastoma tumor. Now, I thought a tumor would be a growth in the brain. And that's what I envisioned: they could do surgery and cut it out like other forms of cancer you hear about.

But I learned differently when we went in to see her. She kept saying, "It's not a big deal."

"Cancer is kind of a big deal," I told her.

"We'll get through it. We'll have surgery," she said.

My brother, sister, and mom's sister (my aunt) were there. She seemed to be in good spirits, so we met the doctor and learned more about what was going on.

He put up the X-ray film. That's when I discovered: a glioblastoma tumor is an extremely aggressive cancer that creates a void in the brain. The tissue is gone, and all they could do at that time was cut around where that void was to try to eliminate the remaining cancer cells.

I remember him putting up that image of the black hole in my mother's brain and how much that impacted me at that moment.

They performed surgery right away, and when she came out, it seemed to have been very successful. I'm hopeful that this is just a bump in the road. She'll take some time to recover and be well in no time.

So we held on to that hope. I was still running the investigation for the accident, still grieving Kieron and Kevin. I had to head back to Pensacola and the work that waited for me.

So we flew back home. They put my mother in hospice, but they often do that to ensure patients get the care they need when recovering from a major surgery like that one, so I wasn't worried.

A few weeks later, I asked, just before Thanksgiving, to go see her, and I took a Blue Jet out to Vegas. I thought it would be great to see her as a Blue Angel.

I landed at the airport, and my sister and one of my mom's friends picked me up.

"Let's go to lunch on the way to the hospital," they said.

"No," I told them. "I didn't come to go to lunch. I came to see Mom. Let's just go."

They dropped me off, and I went to my mom's room. I got to spend some time with her one on one.

We just talked, and she hugged me—one of those warm, incredible hugs that only a mom could give. I sat and held her hand as we watched Oprah on the small television.

Then she turned her head toward me and coughed. And that was it.

I wasn't sure what had happened since I had never experienced that before.

So I called the hospice nurse, and she just turned and looked at me. And that's when I knew she passed. And I just collapsed into the nurse's arms. I wish I could remember her name because she literally embraced me and helped me through one of the most challenging moments of my life. Afterward, I went into the chapel in the hospice facility and sobbed.

That was my October 28, 1999, to November 24, 1999. Here's the insanity in hindsight. I knew that those were monumental events in any person's life. I was also very dedicated to my craft and was very good at compartmentalizing. To be a successful fighter pilot, you have to be able to compartmentalize in the moment and even over the long term. And I have a gift for doing that. And so I separated my emotions from what actually needed to be done. We buried my mother. I mourned deeply then and returned to the team to continue executing my duties as an investigator.

Because for the next three years, my life would be one show after another, and I couldn't afford to take time off and grieve like some people could. I'd been selected as a Blue Angel and had already endured incredible events that might have driven many people to quit, to give up.

But that wasn't one of my choices nor my nature. It was time to get back to work.

8

A NEW YEAR

N ow normally, numbers seven and eight fly around the country to the thirty-six show sites for the upcoming season to do what we call winter visits, to go meet with their show committees and talk about the upcoming shows.

Generally, you'd spend a few weeks in December doing that, but we did not because I was still working on the investigation, which we finally wrapped up in December.

The cause of the accident might never be truly known. "It was a very devastating time," said Cmdr. Pat Driscoll, the Boss, in an interview with CNN. "It's something you don't really put behind you but deal with every day."

"There are so many different pieces, we will never know exactly what happened," said Rear Admiral Michael Bucchi, chief of Naval Air Training, in the same interview.

The most likely culprit, at least as far as we could determine, was a G-forces-related event, and without getting overly technical, that's really all we can say even now.

But because of how long the investigation took to finalize, we did our winter visits in January instead.

The show season starts the second week of March in El Centro and lasts throughout the year. The 2000 season included a show in May, the Department of Defense Joint Services Open House, and Andrew's Air Force Base Air Show, where the Thunderbirds and the Blue Angels were featured in the same event back-to-back.

A lot of the pilots don't like to be number seven because it's a lot of work, and you're kind of a bootstrap for the other six pilots, but I loved it. Essentially my job was to execute all of the logistics for the team. Those included simple things, like how do we get the team from one function to another? Where are they going to sign autographs where the make-a-wish kids so we can visit with them? That was a favorite and humbling team event held every Friday before a show.

And my duties also included making the schedule, like what time do we meet the next day to go to the show? How many rental cars are there? What time do we leave the hotel, and where are we going to eat?

I narrated the show, did all the VIP flights, and even ensured we had gasoline for the generators. I was the Aide de Camp for the team, and I loved it. It meant I was the only guy in the Navy with two F/A-18s assigned to me exclusively to get to wherever I needed. My name was on the side of both of them. And that's how important that role was. But it was very much a customer service role for the rest of the team.

That first year was a great way to be introduced to the culture of service and excellence I would carry with me for the rest of my life.

When you get picked up for the team, you start to be indoctrinated into a new level of attention to detail. We had to have two kinds of pens, and each one has to be in a particular pocket on the shoulder. You also can't talk to people with your sunglasses on.

Your cover has to be worn a certain way. Your zipper has to be to a certain length, and your shoes need a particular shine. Everything is specific and detailed. At the time, you think, God, these people are so anal-retentive. This is ridiculous. But the standards apply to everybody on the team.

This includes all 160 Sailors and Marines that are on the team. But pretty soon, you realize that where your pen sits is essential because that kind of attention to detail and rigor is important in flying, maintaining an aircraft, and it's vital to public relations, foundationally that lays the standards and the groundwork for the team.

To have any culture of that kind of excellence, you have to have a strategic, common goal. Our team motto is, "The Delta always comes first." That meant that we had to get six airplanes in the air, and in order to do that, we did whatever it took.

If I had to stick around and do a maintenance flight right before sunset, then that's what had to be done. If the maintenance personnel or the Marines had to fly a C-130 to

Lemoore, California, to pick up an F/A-18 engine because one of them broke and they would get back at one in the morning, then that's what they did.

Because the next day, we would have six airplanes in the air, no matter what. And so there was a period of time where I thought, "Well, the Delta comes first is kind of putting mission before people."

But that wasn't necessarily true. The people come first because we took care of the team writ large, every single member. As a result, everybody rose to the occasion to ensure that there would be a full Delta no matter what.

We were all so valued and respected that when it came time to do the hard things, you had extra volunteers because everybody wanted to ensure we fulfilled our mission.

You can't claim to be the best in the world and wow the crowd with your precision and excellence if you're a six-airplane team and can only get five airplanes airborne.

That still exists today. If I go to a show, or there's anybody that was on the team, and they have less than six airplanes in the air, then you know it's not good. There can be all reasons why that happens, but you should exhaust all efforts, even to extraordinary lengths, before that ever happens because that's what we do.

Another thing about that year as #7 was talking to people before a show. I always went to breakfast with people before the show, and I enjoyed doing it. I did tons of social stuff; the other guys on the team would say, "you always say yes, you're crazy."

And I said, "Yeah, because most people don't get to meet a

Blue Angel pilot, and when they do, it humanizes the performance. So instead of seeing blue jets, they look at the number 5 jet and go, 'Oh, I know, Scott. I had breakfast with him.'"

It makes it personal. And there's an attachment. When they meet you beforehand, it changes the way they experience the show. They view it much differently than if they meet you afterward in the crowd or in line signing autographs.

During the time I was with the Blues, I went from Lieutenant to Lieutenant Commander. But things got even more exciting when I moved from number 7 to number 6, the opposing solo in 2001, and then to number 5, the lead solo in 2002.

9

CLOSE CALL

T he first year in the Blue Angels, as the number 7, I did the narration and a bunch of other logistical things for the team. In my number 6 year, I was learning to fly for the team.

Keep in mind none of us were new to flying. I had 2200 hours of flight time in the F/A-18. But I had never flown the way the Blue Angels do. And whenever you perform a new maneuver, since you don't do that in a simulator, you brief it really thoroughly first and talk about the risks.

That means you talk through the maneuver, the safety concerns, and how you will do it. We also elevated the safety parameters. Most of the team's maneuvers are at 200 feet above the ground at a speed of 400 knots. January 16, 2001, was the first time I was going to fly the "Bahi." To add a margin of safety, we were going to practice with a hard deck of 2000 feet. 1800 feet above our minimum altitude.

The maneuver was going to be called the Bahi. The idea was that we would come from behind the crowd in a climb, going over them and climbing to about 5000 feet. When we reached that altitude, we would roll inverted and then pull downward toward the ground perpendicular to the earth, then rotate 90 degrees so that we faced each other canopy to canopy.

That was how it was supposed to happen. Then with the other plane in sight, we would radio, "Contact!" which told the other pilot that we saw them.

Number 5 would call "Ready, Hit It," and we would cross, hopefully to the crowd's amazement.

Fortunately, this happened in practice. Remember, we had a hard deck of 2000 feet. On the pull down toward the earth, we erroneously left the power up because we missed a standard operating procedure. Most of the time, you pull the power back when you're in a dive.

So we're accelerating towards the Earth faster than we usually would have been. When you're in the middle of the desert, it's really hard to rotate to 90 degrees perfectly, so we were a little bit canted when we were supposed to face each other. So as I'm looking up to where I expect to see Judge, I don't see him, and he looks up and didn't see me either.

That meant the "contact!" call to identify that we both had a visual of each other didn't happen. The hair on the back of my neck stood up, and I remember thinking, "Wow, I have been pointed at the ground a really long time," So I looked into the heads-up display (HUD) and the altitude reading when I was still 90 degrees perpendicular to the earth, accelerating toward the ground was 1100 feet.

Remember, for safety that day, we set our absolute minimum altitude at 2000 feet. I was 900 feet below that already.

Some key thoughts went through my mind really fast. Option one was that I should eject, but I knew if I ejected, I would have just ended up in the fireball and the crater the F/A-18 crashing would create. The second option was to pull as hard as I could. So I just pulled a solid seven and a half G's and narrowly avoided hitting the ground.

How narrowly? The lowest altitude that the radar altimeter triggered was 27 feet.

Judge was behind me, and I know he was under 100 feet when he pulled up. There's a video of the incident, and you can see how close I come to the ground.

That's because the camera is always on the new guy in these situations. I nearly died, and I have a visual record of it.

I called "knock it off," which is what you say when you want to end whatever maneuver you are doing.

We landed and debriefed what had happened with the entire team so we could all learn from the errors.

My kids were three and one at the time, and I knew I had nearly orphaned them and turned Lisa into a widow.

Keep in mind this was January of 2001. Just over a year earlier, I'd had to investigate the death of Tater and Chicken Bone and deal with my mom's death. And she was the person I thought of as I saw the earth rushing up at me in what I thought might be my last moment on Earth.

As a team, we decided we would not fly that maneuver again. It was too high risk and didn't do much at all to wow the crowd. So that was the last time it was performed.

We also went right back to flying. Judge and I were in our flight suits the next day and up in the air, practicing other maneuvers we would perform throughout the upcoming show season.

There wasn't time to dwell on it. We had a season to prepare for, so we debriefed and disseminated the lessons learned.

The lesson is a simple one. We all face failure, which can nearly kill us in some cases. But we pick ourselves up and learn from our mistakes, execute what we have to do next, and move forward. And that's one-way organizations can get better and embrace a culture of excellence. You brief something and understand it before you try it. But if it doesn't work, you debrief and learn from it, continuing to improve every day.

It's one of the many lessons I learned with the Blues that I would take into my career and that I still use today.

But a little later in 2001, another set of events happened that would change the world forever.

10

SATAN'S KITTENS

September 11, 2001

L ike everyone else, I will never forget where I was on the morning of September 11. I remember that day vividly. I was the number six pilot that year, and we had just finished our morning brief.

Somebody, I don't remember who, said. "Hey, an airplane just hit the World Trade Center."

I remember looking and seeing it on the news and thinking, "Gee, some doctor or dentist crashed his Cessna. Gosh, what a shame."

But we were on timeline and we had to go out and get our practice done just like we did every single day.

Every practice The Blues do is just like a show, from the walk-downs to the salutes and all the elements you see when you attend as an audience member. Just like always, we made our way out to the jets and strapped in.

The diamond taxied out and took off first while myself and Judge, the number five pilot, remained on the ground, ready to launch once they had completed the takeoff.

They started their loop, and just as they reached the top, our maintenance officer called over the radio, "Knock it off, knock it off." Remember, this is what we broadcast when we want to end a maneuver for safety.

The loop, especially the top of the loop, is possibly the worst time in the whole show to call "knock it off." Judge and I held our brakes and waited for orders, wondering what was going on. The diamond came around to land, and we taxied out of the way. Everything was way out of our norms. But we followed procedure, got the airplanes parked, and went back inside to see what this was all about.

During the time since we had started practice and the diamond took off, the second airplane had struck the World Trade Center, the Pentagon had been hit, and the government recognized that we were under attack.

The FAA immediately shut down the airspace over the United States, as no one knew what other aircraft could be out there and what they would do. That meant we, too, were grounded.

Many people don't know that during the Korean War, the Blue Angels shut down as a flight demonstration unit and made up the bulk of the wartime squadron VF-191, known as Satan's Kittens, and went to Korea to join the war effort.

All of the Blue Angels are combat pilots and operational pilots before we join the team.

We just have the opportunity to serve in this recruiting role for a few years. So we immediately developed a plan regarding how rapidly we could make the transition from show ready to combat-ready if needed.

All the publications said 72 hours to turn a Blue Angel jet back into a combat-ready aircraft. We'd have to take out the smoke tanks, which is where the machine gun typically goes and put the weapons back into the aircraft. We immediately shifted out of the airshow pilot mindset and back to operational pilot thinking. We wanted to get in the fight wherever it might happen.

We started the process of coordinating with Boeing and our maintenance teams to determine where the machine guns were stored and how fast we could get them up and ready. We planned to follow the same sequence that had happened during the Korean War: redesignate as Satan's Kittens and deploy within, at the time, we were saying 72 hours. That was enough time to re-paint the jets battle gray.

Everyone was prepared to start that process as soon as we got orders, but as the ensuing weeks passed, we realized nothing was going to happen that rapidly. An active conflict was not starting, at least not the kind we would be involved in quickly.

We didn't fly during that time because we couldn't. But once authorized, we flew out to El Centro and did a few quick refresher flights before the airshow season was scheduled to start again.

We were just north of Dallas at Alliance Field for our first air show back on October 20th and 21st, just over a month after 9/11.

My takeoff maneuver was what we call the low transition high-performance climb split-s. Essentially, I would do a vertical climb, then at 3,000 feet, split-s, and come back down toward the crowd.

It was different that day, though. I did my low transition high-performance climb, and as soon as I split-s, I could see I-35 and the people below. The freeway was shut down, and all the traffic had stopped. People were out of their cars waving these gigantic American flags. The whole crowd line was red, white, and blue. There were hundreds of thousands of people.

I just remember looking down in awe. I mean, the patriotism raging through the country was incredible at that time, and I got to see it from three thousand feet. It's a snapshot I will never ever forget.

The power of that moment is embedded in my mind forever. As Blue Angels, we realized we would not be rushed back into combat. We wouldn't be flying in the skies against the enemy. But what we could do was return to our primary mission, which was representing the warfighters who were preparing to go into battle. We could represent and showcase our armed forces' professionalism, discipline, and expertise.

Because as I said, the Blue Angels are a part of the recruiting arm of the Navy. The patriotism that crossed the country after 9/11 sparked a huge number of enlistments.

When you leave the Blue Angels team, you get a recruiting ribbon. The Air Force pilots from the Thunderbirds get a Distinguished Flying Cross. I'm not jealous. I wear my recruiting ribbon with great pride because we are the best in the world.

But there is more to being a Blue Angel than just flying and representing our Armed Forces well. I had other opportunities, and those came about because I was willing to simply say "yes."

11

POSTERS AND ACTION FIGURES

You work six days a week as a Blue Angel during the show season, pretty much non-stop. Your day off? Monday. So nobody wants to do anything extra, let alone on a Monday. As great as it is, this assignment consumes your life, with shows every weekend, hours of practice flying every week, and constant PR and appearances.

The exception is the number seven on the team, which I had been for the entire previous year. If there is a maintenance flight or something else to do on Mondays, the number seven guy does it . In that position, it can be a long time between days off. So I'd already worked a bunch of Mondays in a row.

Of course, it's exhausting, so often when you're asked to do something, people's instinct is to say, "No."

But I'm not that way. I've been saying "yes" to things my

entire life, and more than once, as you will see, it has resulted in some pretty spectacular opportunities.

The procedure was that when someone wanted something from the Blue Angels team, they would approach the Public Affairs Officer (PAO), and that individual would bring it to what we called the table. The table consisted of the eight aviators at the table and the support officers around the outside, so there would be 16 officers in total. The pilots and support officers would then be asked if anyone wanted to support this request, whatever it was.

One day our PAO, Mike Blankenship, came in and said, "The Naval Aviation Museum needs a Blue Angel Pilot for some pictures."

"What do they need, exactly?" someone asked.

"They need some images, someone to pose for some photos."

I looked around because I'd just moved from number seven to number six, and I had worked Mondays the entire previous year. So to me, it was no big deal. I waited, but nobody raised their hand. So I did.

"Okay," I said. "I'll do it."

I felt like this was a part of our job. So they need a Blue Angel? I'm in.

After all, whatever it is, it's got to be done. It's for the team's betterment, recruiting, and fulfilling our mission statement.

I got the instructions regarding where they wanted me to go and what they wanted me to do. A team of photographers took several pictures of me wearing my helmet and flight suit. It actually turned out to be a pretty cool thing to be a part of, just like a celebrity photo shoot.

As far as I was concerned, that was that. Turns out the photos were used for posters promoting the IMAX film "The Magic of Flight," and because I said yes, my image was everywhere promoting the film.

At one point, the poster even hung in the Naval Aviation Museum, and it was huge, 20 feet by 40 feet. My kids took pictures of it when they went to Pensacola after they joined the Navy, and there it was. And they told their friends, "There's a wall of my dad."

Then, as is true with anything that brings attention to you rather than someone else, other people on the team expressed some jealousy afterward.

They said things like, "Oh, man, you're all over with that poster."

"I didn't know I was going to be the poster," I told them. "Or part of something that was that big of a deal either." The truth was, I volunteered when no one else would, and this time it happened to turn out okay.

But the poster was only the start. Next, another opportunity came along, and you'd think some of the other pilots would have learned. But I had another chance to say "yes." Mike came to the table with another request.

"Hey, look, we have this opportunity. There's a company called Blue Box Toys out of Hong Kong, and they need a Blue Angel flight suit because they're going to create a Blue Angel action figure. You know, one just like the George Bush action figure from when he landed on the carrier."

I looked around, and once again, no one raised their hand. Nobody wanted to give up their flight suit. I had tons of Blue Angel flight suits. They weren't really mine anyway. They belonged to the United States Government.

So I volunteered again and said, "Sure, you can have one of my flight suits. Take it."

I brought it in, and they shipped it off to Hong Kong. I thought that was the end of it. Fast forward four or five months later, and Mike Blankenship approached, not the table, but me this time.

"Hey, the Blue Box toy company wants a bunch of digital images of your face." At that time, digital photography was relatively new, and high-definition photography was a leading-edge tech

So I did as I was told and went to the studio. The company took sixteen pictures of my head from various angles and shipped that off. It didn't take much time, and I didn't think much about it.

The next thing I knew, they had created this "Intake" doll or rather Blue Angel action figure. I have one of the prototypes that looked just like me.

The final product doesn't look anything like that, though, because this toy would not be marketable with my face on it, so they changed it a bit. But my picture is on the side of the box, and it is labeled "the Scott Kartvedt Number 5 solo pilot Blue Box Toys action figure." They subsequently also made a watch and Blue Angel helmets in plastic cases. They were created for collectors, and the helmets all said "Intake" on the back, just like my Blue Angel helmet.

And when the pilots that wouldn't give their flight suit or wouldn't give up a Monday to go have pictures taken said things like, "Oh, you know, you got a doll. You're always just watching out for Intake. You always just look out for yourself."

But when I heard these comments, I thought, "God's honest truth is, it doesn't have anything to do with that. I happen to turn or walk through open doors. And if there is an opportunity on the other side, great. I like to say yes to opportunity."

But there are so many people in their lives that won't walk through the open door. They predetermine an answer because it's unknown, and they often answer "no" for themselves. And then they get upset when things don't turn out, or they miss an opportunity.

"Oh, I have a great idea," people will say. "But my boss will shoot it down. So they decide before they even ask that "no" will be the answer. The boss never even got to hear about it. And that's where the idea, possibly a good one, died.

But sometimes, you just need to try something and see what happens. Even if you are in a really good place, you might want to see what else is around the corner. Say "yes" and allow good things to happen. It doesn't always work that way, but good happens often. Say "Yes!"

12

MAKING SPACE AND BUSTING MYTHS

I was number Five on the Blue Angels team when I applied to NASA to be an astronaut. I thought that would be amazing, and I still think so. I certainly think I have the capability to be an astronaut.

But what I don't have is the technical engineering degree NASA is usually looking for. And while I have flown literally thousands of hours, I haven't been to test pilot school.

Part of the reason I didn't go to test pilot school? I consider myself an operator, meaning I can operate machinery. I am not a mechanic and want to do about five minutes of paperwork for every flight hour. But test pilots do about three days of paperwork for every one hour of time they spend flying. That might be a slight exaggeration, but it has some truth. They're usually big-time academics, trained engineers, and often even hold a doctorate degree.

Anyhow, NASA was accepting applications in the 2002

timeframe, and so with the same mentality I used when I approached the Blues, I applied. I put my package together, I got the recommendations I needed to have, and I went and took the physical.

Keep in mind I did this whole thing while I was the number five pilot on the Blues and working a grueling schedule already.

Max McCoy, slot pilot #4 at the time, callsign "Pepper" and now Rear Admiral Max McCoy, said, "Intake. I don't know why you're doing this. It's a waste of time. The only way you're going to space is in a cage so that they can study you."

Honestly, that was a pretty legit response. Technically, I was not qualified to be an astronaut.

At the time, I responded with a huge laugh because Pepper is hilarious.

But everyone was right when they said, "You don't have an engineering degree. You're not a test pilot." Those two things were almost concrete requirements if you wanted to go to space.

"I get it," I said. "But NASA will never hear about Scott Kartvedt and call me up and ask me to be an astronaut. The only way for me to even try to become one is to apply. And they can only bring good news.

"Because if they call or send my application back and say, 'Guess what? You're not an astronaut,' well, I'm already not an astronaut. It hasn't cost me anything but a little bit of time to apply. Then I'll know for sure."

This is part of my mentality and my overall approach to

life. I'm not afraid to fail. I have no problem saying, "Hey, I applied to be an astronaut. They didn't pick me." Because just like when I said people don't take their ideas to their boss because they assume he will say "no," most people would never even apply to NASA because they assume they won't be picked.

Even if you are qualified, the odds are incredibly small. In all of human history, only just over 600 people have orbited the Earth.

But I took a chance, and through that application and my interest in NASA, I met some fantastic people, including Captain Bill Reedy, an astronaut and a shuttle mission commander. He attended the Blue Angels' final show in Pensacola and our big end-of-season party.

The following day, I got up and went with him to see a shuttle launch and meet a bunch of people who worked for NASA, and I would never have had that opportunity if I didn't actually apply to join the program and hadn't asked for help during that process. So when I'm 60, 70, 80, or on my deathbed, I won't have any regrets wondering whether they would have picked me or not. I tried, and that's more than most people ever do.

Like being an astronaut, there is only one way to become a part of the Blue Angels: you have to apply. Occasionally, the spouse of another pilot who was not on the team would approach one of our wives.

They would approach Lisa or one of the other wives and say, "Oh, yeah, you know, the Blue Angels called and asked my husband if he wanted to join the team, and he was going to do it. But you know, family was really important to him, and he wanted to stay home."

And our wives would smile and say, "Yeah, I'm sure he did what was right for him."

But let me make it perfectly clear. The Blue Angels work the same way NASA does. The Blue Angels have never called anybody and told them that they had been selected for the team unless they applied. The first requirement is you have to want to be on the team. It is a lot of time away from home, and some sacrifices come with it.

Now, what probably did happen in those cases is that one of the other Blue Angel pilots or I talked to someone who expressed interest in applying to be on the team.

Let's say somebody named Jim, a Navy pilot, approached one of us.

"Hey, I'm thinking about applying to join the Blues."

And anyone on the team might say, "That's a great idea. I think you'd be a terrific addition to the team."

That's not the same as applying to join the team, interviewing, or getting selected. I encouraged anybody that said they were interested in the team to apply and told them that they would be a great addition to the team regardless of their background.

But that's because I wanted them to go for it if that was their dream, the same as when I applied to the team and even to NASA. But they had to act and step through that door, not knowing what the answer on the other side might be.

Many didn't want to face the possibility of "no" rather than considering the possibility we would say "yes." Some wanted the name and the glory but not the responsibility. And others might even be embarrassed if they tried and failed.

One other thing you have to understand about the Blue Angels. It isn't a career. You serve one tour, two or three years, with the Blues.

You come from the fleet when you join the team, and when you're done with your tour, you return to the fleet.

And the time had come for me to return.

13

THE FINAL SHOW

Is joining the Blue Angels good for a Navy career? Well, perhaps now more than it was when I was with them. It all depends on career timing. There was a period of time where if you got selected late, the time you spent in the Blues could make you late for your department head timing, which might actually harm your career. Because if you know anything about military careers, just like civilian careers, it's all about how many years you have in when you reach a certain level, which also relates to how much time you have left in your career.

Eventually, timing mattered less as attitudes started to shift. The Navy began acknowledging the commitment and sacrifice required to be on the team.

Remember, the Blue Angels pilots rotate off the team in groups of three. At the end of your tour, only one pilot would be ranked number one. Only a single pilot of those returning to the fleet would get a "ticket," essentially your choice of assignments, and the other two pilots wouldn't, even though all three put in the same time and effort.

Finally, the Navy realized that, like Top Gun, the Blue Angels is a different ballgame. Similar to the Top Gun instructors, in which case, if you're number 30 of 30 Top Gun instructors, you're still number one in most places. If you're number three of three, leaving the Blues to return to a unit, you're still career competitive and exceptionally capable.

Anyway, when I reached my final show as a Blue Angel, it was a bittersweet moment. Remember my friend, Bob, now Bob "Kelvin" Brust? The one who started with me on this whole crazy ride? Well, he flew F-15s in the Air Force and was in Japan at the time of my last show in 2002.

I called him and said, "Look, Bobby, if you're gonna fly with me while I'm a Blue Angel, it has to happen right now."

Of course, he wanted to do it, so he flew out from Japan and met me in Pensacola at the site of our last show. During my final practice, he got to jump in my back seat and fly the demonstration with me.

It was a special moment for both of us. We'd both gone on to fulfill our dreams of being fighter pilots, and now we were both in Blue Angel number 5 for my final practice.

Following that special moment, we went on to do the show. Two days later, during my final landing, my last flight as Blue Angel number 5, as my wheels hit the ground, I began to sob. I literally felt my shoulders slump.

I had survived even though I had nearly died. I had made it through three years of sometimes seemingly endless air shows, and successfully. I didn't realize until that moment the burden that I was carrying from that initial accident investigation and the overwhelming loss not only of Kieron and Kevin but also of my mother at the very beginning of my Blue Angel tour. And so when we taxied in and parked, other teammates saw that my eyes were red, and I had been crying.

"Oh, we knew you were going to miss it," they told me. And they weren't wrong. They knew I loved being a Blue Angel.

I just smiled and laughed and said, "Yeah, I'm going to miss it. It has been quite the experience."

I talked about the need, as a pilot, to be able to compartmentalize, but sometimes you have to let that dam break and deal with the emotions you couldn't deal with at the time.

It's interesting how the brain functions to allow you to continue working and living and doing what you have to do, and then it recognizes when it's okay to re-emote all of those feelings.

If we fast forward for a moment, during my command tour, I could understand the human factors people who worked for me were going through, whether it was relationship-wise, sick parents, sick kids, sick dogs, or whatever life threw at them. Sometimes, it's okay just to stop and feel and live before the next chapter starts.

That experience gave me a wider aperture of empathy and understanding of the importance of mental health. And that sometimes, we have to allow ourselves to break because the human body and mind can only take so much.

That final flight with the Blue Angels meant that part of my naval career had ended, and it was time to go to war.

14

RETURNING TO THE FLEET

I t's important to note here that I had not been through what they call the fleet replacement squadron since 1994. That's where they refresh you on tactics and weapons, both air-to-ground and air-to-air. By now, it was very early 2003, and weapons and systems had come a long way in almost a decade.

This was what they call in a Naval officer's career my Department Head tour. In corporate speak, I acted in a Navy role similar to middle management. In my case, I acted as the safety officer for the squadron, due in no small part to the safety and accident investigation experience I brought to the table.

When I got my orders, they told me, "Hey, war is about to kick off over in Iraq, and the unit you're going to is out in the eastern Mediterranean. We're just going to send you to do your carrier qualifications, and then you're going to join them in combat."

"Okay, I'm thrilled to join the conflict because that is our profession," I said. "And I have no issue with that. But I haven't been trained in laser-guided weapons, the GPS-guided weapons, the Joint Direct Attack Munitions (JDAM), or any of the new air to air weapons."

"Yeah, but you'll get that training when you get over there," they told me. "Plus, you're a Blue Angel."

"Well, if you want me to fly upside down at 200 feet over the Iraqis to music, I'm your guy," I told them. "There's nobody better. But if you want me to engage against them and neutralize them, I could use some weapons refreshment training."

"Yeah, don't worry about it," they told me again. "You'll get what you need at your squadron."

I wasn't confident that was the best idea, but I followed my orders.

A Greyhound, a transport plane that lands on a carrier, took me out to the ship. I joined the night strike team on the *USS Roosevelt* in the eastern Mediterranean. At the time, they were off the coast of Cyprus. The next day, we did one flight off the carrier as a warmup, and I felt pretty good.

On that first flight off the *Roosevelt,* we went through what we call the weapon switchology on our secure flight radios. Those are the techniques used to employ the weapons, something I hadn't done in a long time, and as I mentioned, never with some of the newer technology. The following day, we did it again on a secure KY58 radio over

Turkey for an hour and a half, then turned right, south into Iraq. If I had to engage, I was as ready as I would get.

We were there for eight weeks. There wasn't a lot of air-to-air resistance there, and one one flight, me and my wingman, a guy named "Newman," were assigned to a kill box in Northern Iraq.

Nothing was happening in that area at that time because the whole push of the battle had moved south rapidly, as you might recall. And I thought, you know, let's go where the action is.

So we just turned south and headed towards Baghdad.

"That area's not where we're assigned," Newman argued.

"Yeah, but that's where the action is," I told him. "So let's go ."

On the way, we were talking to all the joint tactical controllers on the ground. From time to time, we got lit up by anti-aircraft weapons, but it was dark, and we had our night vision goggles on. That meant you could look out and see a missile coming at you if there was one.

What the Iraqis would do is light you up with the radar just to get you to defend so that you couldn't employ your weapons. And I remember Newman getting lit up and going into his surface-to-air missile defense maneuvers.

"Newman," I remember saying. "There's nothing coming up. You're depleting all of your energy."

Now maybe that was dumb of me because there could have been something, and I might not have seen it. But with the night vision goggles, you could see the anti-aircraft artillery and surface-to-air missles if they actually fired. You can see everything at night, which was a huge advantage for us.

Once he got comfortable watching for threats, we made it down to Baghdad with all of the lights. We could see the battle raging below. It was really wild.

Because of our air superiority, we met our objective way ahead of schedule. There just wasn't much of a defense at that time. The squadron I joined had already been at sea for quite some time, and I just happened to join them for Shock and Awe.

We departed the war in late May, so I was not out to sea that long. When we were done and soon to be headed home, we pulled into Cartagena, Spain for seven days. I'm sure you've seen Pirates of the Caribbean, where they pull into Tortuga. If you want to enjoy the spoils of war with sailors, who are now partying like pirates because they just won a war, give them a week in a port like Cartagena.

It was just absolutely unbelievable. We felt like the conquering heroes, and we acted like it, too, in typical Navy style. Then we sailed back across the Atlantic, back to Virginia Beach and Norfolk.

The war was still going on. But in the second half of 2003, not too much happened, and it looked like I might actually be home for a while.

So in 2004, I decided to do something I'd wanted to do for a long time but never had the opportunity to do before.

IRONMAN TO ADMIRAL'S AIDE

W hat had I always wanted to do? Well, when I was nineteen, I wrote a list of nine things I wanted to do before I died. And an Iron Man was one of them. I knew that I had the opportunity, but it felt like this might be the only summer it would be possible. The kids were a little older, and I was flying all the time still, but I felt like I could manage the training I would need to do.

I was still relatively young, at 36, and I had recently done a small Iron Man with my friend Andy "Woody" Lewis.

"You know, that was a lot of fun. I think I want to do a full Ironman."

"Intake," he said, "That's a whole lot different than the one we just did."

"Yeah, but I can do it," I told him. "I've got the time and energy to train."

I decided this when it was a bit late to register for the

Lake Placid Iron Man. All the slots were full. But not one to take no for an answer, I called the committee and said, "Hey, I'm a veteran. I know the race is already full. But this is the only time I'm going to have to do it. Is there any way you can make an exception?"

And they said, "Sure."

Once again, proving that it never hurts to ask. So I signed up. Andy Lewis was signed up to do it, also. So we planned to do it together. We went up there with our families on July 25, 2004.

The way it broke down for me was: in the swim, I did pretty well. The bike portion I was thrilled with. The run I survived.

I was a swimmer and water polo player. So the swim didn't bother me, and I wasn't worried about my ability to do it. I trained on the bike a lot because I wanted to be really comfortable on it. I wasn't a huge cyclist.

But I had run a bunch of marathons, or a handful of them anyway. I ran cross country at Pepperdine when I was in college. So I rested on my laurels when it came to the run, telling myself, "I'm a pretty good runner."

What I didn't consider is that after 112 miles on a bike, I wasn't that good of a runner.

The first 13 miles of the marathon were brutal. The Lake Placid course is really unique in that the way it's laid out means there are two laps for the swim, two laps for the bike, and two laps for the run. So your spectators can see you halfway through each part of the event.

Halfway through the run, I stopped next to my wife.

She asked, "How's it going?"

"Well, I'm not doing so hot. I have no idea how long this next 13 miles will take."

But shortly after that, all of the nutrition that I ate on the bike kicked in, and the calories I absorbed gave me new energy. I was very disciplined with what I ate along the way. I actually had a negative split on the run and felt pretty good as I neared the finish. But here's the crazy part.

Andy and I had served together before, and he and had gone to Iraq together in both 1996 and 2003. I didn't see him the whole race except once on the bike when he passed me. And then, no kidding, the last 200 yards of the run. I rounded a left turn, and he was right there. And we ended up finishing together stride for stride, crossing the finish line after 12 hours, 17 minutes, and 39 seconds.

That was my summer of 2004, the year I checked a major item off my bucket list. When 2005 came, it was time to go back to war.

During Operation Iraqi Freedom, there wasn't a lot of air resistance, as we had pretty much wiped that out already. There were a lot of IEDs, and we spent significant time looking for and destroying them.

I had to blow up one building in Syria because the enemy was using it for weapons storage and coming down the Tigris River valley into Baghdad. Several individuals ran out as the building was on fire and falling down around them, and I was able to neutralize them with the help of a Marine sniper who was on the ground.

But halfway through that deployment, I received a new challenge and a new set of orders.

In Navy speak, I had my "ticket punched" and got an incredible job offer.

Admiral Timothy J. Keating asked me to be his Aide de Camp.

The way the offer came was this: we were at an event, and he approached me.

"Hey, I've got a question for you. Do you want me to be my Aide de Camp? It's a horrible job, but it's yours if you want it."

"Well, I don't really like horrible jobs," I said. "But I heard you're a great man to work for. So I'll do it."

"Not so fast," he said, it's a lot of work and a lot of travel, and you're just coming off deployment. Why don't you go talk to Lisa about it, and see what she says."

Anytime you get to work for a four-star, it's generally a pretty incredible opportunity. Some four stars are better to work for than others, and I knew Admiral Keating from before, and he had an incredible reputation. I also knew from what Lisa and I had been through before that she would say yes.

The same way I said yes.

So I embarked on what I didn't know yet would be a Ph.D. course in leadership. This was partly because Admiral Keating knew that he was grooming the next leaders of the Navy, building continuity with leaders he thought would have the potential to go on and lead at much higher levels than where they were now.

And that's precisely what I intended to do. So in December of 2005, my Navy career changed direction yet again.

16

NEXT LEVEL LEADERSHIP

In December 2005, I joined Admiral Keating's staff. It was the experience of a lifetime. I joined him every-where he went, every meeting, and all along the way, he quietly taught me lessons, many simply through his example.

Whenever he had a meeting, I got to sit in. That included meetings with the Chairman of the Joint Chiefs, General Peter Pace, at the time and meetings with Secretary Rums-feld. For me, it was just unbelievable.

I didn't have a speaking part, but I listened to some of the greatest leaders of our time. And we'd have meetings with the director of the FBI, the head of the CIA, and a variety of congressmen and senators. Seeing how these leaders inter-acted with one another, how they discussed issues, and even what they discussed at what level taught me a lot about how things worked at a command level, not only in the Navy but the nation.

We were in Northern Command, which is all North American defense. While we were in Washington much of the time, in the two years I was with him, we went on 67 trips in total. He welcomed me into meetings with the Chinese Chief of Naval Operations and many other international leaders as well.

It was a Ph.D. in leadership because when we would get in the armored suburban after these meetings, I could ask questions and talk to him about what had just been discussed. He solicited my advice even and would ask me what I thought. To be a trusted confidant for that period of time was great, but it also taught me that no matter what level of leadership you have reached, the opinions of others do matter regardless of their rank in relation to yours.

The other interesting thing is often, as an aide, you'd have to chase the person you're working for. But Admiral Keating was different.

I'd race next to him as he walked around headquarters at first and ask, "Can I get you anything, sir? What do you need?"

"No, I'm just doing a walkabout," he'd tell me.

He interacted well with people, no matter who they were, from security details to other members of the military and civilians alike.

The first week I was with him, we were walking through the Pentagon. We're coming up on a door, and there were some four stars that would stop short of the doors so that somebody would open it for them, and they could walk through. Some expected someone to run ahead so they wouldn't even have to break stride to enter a building.

I knew that because some of the other aides had told me about these things they had to do.

We were walking up to a door, and I said, "Hey, I gotta ask, you want me to run ahead and open the door? Do you want me to get it for you? Do you want me to walk on your right side?

"How about we do this?" he said. "Whoever gets to the door first opens it."

That was Admiral Keating, just incredibly practical. He wanted me to support him, which was my job, but he didn't treat me as his servant.

As we walked, if there was any trash on the ground, in his headquarters, or at the Pentagon, whether in a building or outside, he would stop and pick it up and then walk over and throw it away.

The first time I saw him do it, I didn't really catch what happened. The second time I said, "You should give me that. I'll get it for you."

"Yeah, you can get the next one," he said. "It's our building. It's our Pentagon."

It's such a simple thing to do. It changed the way that everybody worked in the building because if the four-star Admiral can take the time to pick up a piece of trash, so can everybody.

It was all about attention to detail, the little things. I took that into command when I was put in a place of leadership. And whenever I would be on the carrier, I would stop and pick up trash if I saw it. I had people that worked for me, as I was leaving, they'd say, look, I saw you pick up trash, and I didn't understand it at first, but now I get it, you know, and so I can't walk by trash without picking it up anymore.

Anybody that would ask, "Why did you pick up the trash?

I'd answer, "Because it's our ship. If nobody picks up the trash, then we're just going to have a ship full of trash. But if everybody picks up the trash, then we're going to have a really clean ship. And it's going to be a pleasure to live on. So I pick it up."

There is one really funny story. As an Aide de Camp, I would get him a Diet Coke with lime wherever we went.

I would have that ready wherever meetings were. If someone asked what kind of beverage Admiral Keating would like to have on hand, that's what I would tell them.

One day, we're in the Pentagon, and he was getting ready to go into a room called The Tank, which is where the Chairman of the Joint Chiefs and all the four stars get briefed and where really high-level decisions are made.

Admiral Keating worked as the director of the Joint Staff, so he knew all of the people who worked there. And we walked into the tank, and it's just he and I, and this enlisted sailor comes up and says, "Hey, Admiral, do you want a Diet Dr. Pepper?

"God, I'd love a Diet Dr. Pepper."

"What?" I said. "I've been working with you for a year. What are you talking about? All you ever drink is Diet Coke with lime."

"No, I love Diet Dr. Pepper," he told me. "But one time, I

went into a meeting, and somebody offered me a Diet Coke with Lime. And I said sure, that sounds good. Now on my prep sheet that goes to all the commands we're visiting. It says the Admiral prefers Diet Coke with lime, but I actually love Diet Dr. Pepper."

The lesson was that sometimes you need to ask more questions. Because of one meeting, it became assumed that Admiral Keating preferred Diet Coke with lime. But that assumption was far from universal, and with a simple question, I could have known what he really liked much sooner.

He had some great sayings that turned into advice that would shape my career. One was "Always underreact so that you don't take any emotion into making an important decision."

I think about that often and use it as a guiding principle always to underreact. Another thing he taught was, "If something is going bad, and there's bad news, just tell me what is happening."

"First off, any information you bring me is just news," he said. "I will determine whether it is good or bad. So just bring me the information. If it is bad, Intake, do you think it's better to put out a fire when it's a spark or when it's an inferno?"

"A spark, I said.

"Bring me bad news early, he said. "That way, we can fix it.

And so I say the same thing, I took that into my command leadership tours. And I still use that. If there's bad news, don't feel bad about bringing the news. I'll determine whether it's good or bad. And if it is bad, tell me early.

I applied that to raising our kids. I'd tell them, "Hey, if you make a bad decision, let me know. So that I can help you navigate through it. Don't try to hide and cover it up because it's only going to amplify and get worse. Both of those were really great lessons I've applied my entire life.

Another great piece of advice came out of a meeting called the Defense Senior Leadership Conference, the DSLC. They had it twice a year for every four star in the military at the Pentagon.

He came out of one of the meetings, and they were in there for hours.

"Admiral, what do you say in those meetings?" I asked him.

"As little as possible," he said. That was his way of saying, "I listen and consider and think."

"There are some guys that go in there and won't give up the microphone," he said. "Because by God they have so much opinion and thought. But that's not generally viewed as sound. So big ears, little mouth. And listen before you speak."

Those were all, and still are pretty lasting leadership lessons. And I'm still in contact with him. He has been a remarkable guiding Light for my kids. He helped get them into the Naval Academy.

That being said, he made a very clear point when I left. "Look, I was an Aid de Camp to a gentleman by the name of Admiral William J. Crowe, who went on to be the Chairman of the Joint Chiefs. He told me, 'Look, don't call and ask for favors once you leave.' So, I didn't," he told me. "So I will tell you the same thing, Intake. Don't call and ask for favors."

He wasn't trying to say that he wouldn't help me. He was trying to say that's not the way it works. Don't just call to ask favors because we worked together once. Don't think of it like, "Oh, yeah. Well, I've got an Admiral I can call to fix this."

He was far more interested in the relationship we developed. I still consider him a mentor and good friend. I text him. On occasion, we go back and forth. He's interested in Wyatt and Nick and always asks about Lisa.

That was fifteen years ago that we worked together. My kids even text him and keep him up to date on their careers.

When my oldest son finished his carrier qualifications, he had texted Admiral Keating to let him know he was going to the ship. Keating is quite simply a remarkable guy.

As it would turn out, my tour with him ended on December 7, 2007. I joked with him that it would be a day that would live in infamy for more than one reason now since I would no longer be his aide. Two years later, in 2009, he retired from active duty in the Navy after 38 years of service.

It was time for me to move on in my path toward Naval Command and to apply those leadership lessons I'd learned.

But while I'd had a Ph.D. course, it wasn't time to call me Dr. Intake. I still had a lot to learn.

17

A NEW X.O

O nce I left Admiral Keating's staff, I headed for my first command, VFA-83, in Virginia Beach. When you get selected for command, many people want to go to the best squadrons because squadrons have reputations. I wasn't inclined to do that, though.

I don't know if I wanted to get into an average or below-average squadron, but I wasn't afraid to. Part of the reason is that it provides an opportunity to create a culture of excellence and to bring a squadron that might be struggling up to a higher standard. It was the first opportunity for me to really be the one who instigated and developed that culture in others, and I was eager to do so.

When you first show up in your command tour, you start as the XO, or second in command. The CO was a gentleman named Paul "Dorf" Olin. He was a quieter guy, a little bit more of an introvert, very thoughtful, and a former Top Gun instructor.

As you can imagine by now, I am a little bit more boisterous and an extrovert. He understood that I had my strengths, and he had his. So he just cut me loose as long as I kept him informed about anything I might be doing.

When I showed up at Strike Fighter Squadron 83, the Rampagers, the personnel were pretty lax regarding military standards. I joined them when they were in Fallon, Nevada, and a few of the guys had wrinkled uniforms, boots that weren't polished, pins out of place, covers worn improperly, and things like that.

To address this, I went and bought a bunch of shoe polish and called all the pilots to the ready room. I picked out a few of the pilots with the worst boots.

I asked them to join me up front.

"Here's your award for the worst boots in the unit," I told them, presenting each of them with a new can of shoe polish. "From now on, everyone needs their boots polished to Navy standard. Our sailors follow your example, so let's set a great one."

Many XOs make the mistake of showing up and doing their XO tour, probably 12 to 18 months, and not doing a lot to change the culture, instead waiting until they become the CO. That tour consists of another 12-15 months. It's not enough time to make the greatest impact on the unit because, on average, it takes at least a year to change the culture.

When I looked at what was happening in this unit, I met

with Dorf, and I outlined what I wanted to do and how I wanted to do it in order to instill the culture of excellence I had come to expect.

"Yeah, absolutely," he said. "Go for it."

One of the first things I did when we were back in Virginia Beach and in our squadron spaces was to go on a tour of the enlisted areas, essentially where the squadron lived.

One of the first things I noticed was the condition of the enlisted men's bathroom.

For one thing, it was small. There were only two stalls, two urinals, and two sinks. One stall wasn't functioning, one urinal didn't work, and both paper towel holders were ripped off the wall. Only one sink had running water.

I grabbed the Master Chief, the senior enlisted person in the squadron, and asked him, "Hey, what's going on here?"

"I know it's a mess, XO, but we've got a requisition order to get this fixed," he told me. "Facilities just hasn't responded with an ETA."

"This is unsat. This doesn't work. You know, if there are 250 People in the squadron, and there is just one toilet, one urinal, and only one place to wash your hands, that's not good enough."

"Well, you know, we've called over to the Facilities Management Group," he said. "But nothing's happening, and we haven't gotten an answer."

"Give me the number," I told him.

I went upstairs, called the facilities group, and got their Maintenance Lead on the phone.

"Hey, how's it going?" I said. "I'm Scott Kartvedt, the new Executive Officer over at VF 83. I just wanted to introduce myself."

"How's everything going?" he asked.

"Great," I said.

"I'm glad you called. Thanks for that. Because my job is managing the facilities. You know, heads, beds, and things like that, and I'm here to help."

"That's good. Because I think there is something you can help me out with right away."

"Yes, sir. What would that be?"

"First, let me ask you a quick question," I said.

"Sure," he said. "Shoot."

"How many people are in your family?" I asked.

"I'm married. I've got three kids."

"How big is your house?"

"That's a weird question, XO."

"Yeah, I know. But I'm just curious. Is it, you know, three bedrooms, two baths?"

"Yeah, it actually is a three-bedroom, two-and-a-half bath," he answered, sounding even more puzzled. "It's in a pretty decent neighborhood."

"Man, that must be nice," I said.

"It is," he answered.

"Well, my family is made up of the two-hundred and fifty sailors here at the squadron. And I have one bathroom with one working toilet and one functioning urinal. And you have five people in your family and three toilets?"

"Y-y-y-es," he said, probably knowing where I was going

with this.

"Do you think that we could get that fixed?"

"Yes, it's on our list," he told me.

"There's a requisition in," I told him and told him how long it had been since it was filed. "I need it fixed. And I want you to tell me when you can fix it."

"We'll be over this week."

"Okay, great. When?"

Two days later, a couple of guys were working on fixing the toilet and the urinal, and the sink.

Once that was being put right, I pulled an Admiral Keating.

I went down there to check on the work being done and the progress. Because there were no paper towel dispensers, and nobody really took care of the bathrooms, people would walk by and dry their hands with towels ripped from big rolls that sat on the side of the non-functioning sink. The wastebasket was full, but they would just try to throw their trash in anyway. Of course, it would just hit the pile in the overfull can and fall on the floor.

As a result, trash littered the floor, and it was filthy like it had not been cleaned in a really long time.

So I walked into maintenance control, where there was another Senior Master Chief and his crew.

"Hey, can I get a dustpan and a broom?" I asked a sailor.

"Oh, yeah, no problem," she said. "Just a minute."

She went and got a dustpan and a broom, and she handed them to me just like I asked.

The E-9 in the room looked at her and then at me. "Sir,

what are you doing with that?"

"I'm going to clean the bathroom," I told him.

"No, no, no. We'll do that, sir. No need for you to do it."

"Come with me," I said. I gestured for him to follow me and walked down the hallway. He followed.

When we got there, I opened the bathroom door.

"Apparently, you won't clean the bathroom," I said. "Or at least you haven't been doing it. But I will."

And I got down on my hands and knees and started cleaning the enlisted men's bathroom. And I cleaned all the paper towels off the floor. I packed up he wastebasket, tied off the trash bag, and put a new one in. I swept the floor, putting all the debris in the dustpan and dumping it into the new liner.

By this time, all kinds of people of all ranks were standing around watching the new XO clean the bathroom.

"How can we help?" several of them asked.

I stood and dusted off my uniform. "You can help by keeping it this way all the time. Because if you don't, then I will," I told them. "Because I care about the health and welfare of our Sailors."

I wasn't trying to make a point to show I was in charge or step on anyone's toes. I truly cared. If nobody else was going to keep things clean, then I was.

Right after that, we got the toilets fixed. The sinks were fixed. The bathroom stayed clean. And that was just the bathroom.

It turned out there was a lot more work to do, too. The enlisted bathroom was just a symptom of a larger problem.

18

TAKING COMMAND

E ven before I took command, I discovered another issue: the awards board.

Every unit has one. There are awards for Sailor of the Quarter, Sailor of the Month, and other similar awards. The award winner usually has their name added to the plaque under that place on the board, and a photo of them would be placed in a holder above their name. But in this unit, there was a problem.

The first time I walked by, and saw that in the last three quarters, there were no pictures in the holders on the board. It was blank.

So I asked the Master Chief, "Where are the pictures? The last three quarters don't have them."

"Sorry about that," he said. "The printer doesn't work a lot of the time, and it's hard to get those up sometimes or even find the time to corner the sailor and take a picture."

"I don't care what you've done before; there's no excuse for this. I don't want to hear about the camera or the printer," I told him. "I'm going to give you till the end of the week. You can't have an awards board and give an award and then not have a picture in the frame."

I knew how it felt. Imagine winning Sailor of the Quarter for the second quarter of 2008. You walk by the board on day one, and your picture is not on the board. Okay, maybe you'd give your unit some grace, but by day seven, quite honestly, you are rightfully upset. Because the squadron leaders not putting up the picture shows that you don't care and acknowledging your sailors is unimportant to you.

And it's true. Because if nobody cared enough to take a picture, print it, and put it on the board, then the "award" doesn't mean a thing. It made me truly angry because I knew I did care, and I wanted the rest of the leadership to care, too.

"Sorry. I didn't think—"

"What it says to the sailors is, 'Here's your award. We don't really care about you.' And we do care about our sailors. So get the pictures in there. If we have to buy a new photo printer, get one. If we have to buy a new camera, fine."

"Of course," he said. "I'm on it."

"By the end of the week, I want this board up to date, period. From now on, the day of the award, the picture goes in. Are there any questions on what the expectation is?"

So we got the awards board set up, and then we got the bathroom squared away. And then we started going around taking pictures of the sailors at work. I would blow up the best of these photos into posters and hang them around the squad spaces. We would change them out about every six weeks when we had a new poster ready.

When I would take the old poster down, I would find the most prominent sailor in the photo, and then I would just sign it and add a personal message. "Thanks for your hard work in the squadron. You make it a better place, XO." Then I would give it to them. And then we'd hang a new picture.

I would do that on a rotational basis. When you call a sailor and say, "Hey, we took this picture of your work, and I just want to give it to you. I signed it to say thanks." They're motivated to do well without even giving them an actual award.

By the time I was in command after 15 months as XO, we had to turn sailors away because they wanted to be in our squadron. We valued and cared for our people.

A sailor approached me one day and said, "There are guys from the other squadrons using our bathroom. It's wrong."

"No, it's not wrong. It's awesome," I told him. "Let them use it because they know that we care."

Once, we were raising money for a squadron Christmas party while we were at sea.

"Hey, look," I said. "I will auction off a day of my work to any one of the divisions or departments in the squadron. I'll work with you and do your job right alongside you for an entire day."

Basically, what I outlined was that whoever raised the most money would win a day of my labor.

All of the sailors in the squadron worked hard, and we raised a lot of money for our party.

The group who won is called the troubleshooters, and they work up on the deck of the carrier. When a plane breaks, they'll run down to the storage room, pick up a part, run it back up, and install it. They all wear heavy tool pouches, so they have all the tools they need to fix a problem quickly. Since they won, I showed up at 7 a.m. with the day shift and worked through the entire day with them.

"Hey, Skipper, you know, thanks for coming up," they said several times throughout the day. "You can go now."

"No," I said. "You paid for a day. And so I'm going to work with you all day. That was the deal."

As the day shift turned into the night shift, they said again, "Okay, Skipper, you know, our shift is over. So you can go now."

"A day is a 24-hour period, and the night shift people paid too," I told them.

I worked my tail off next to all of them. I was on the deck of the carrier for 16 hours. I finished up at 11 o'clock. It was a monstrous day. But the word spread that I had stayed through both the day shift and night shift. The fact that I had worked all that time increased the respect and admiration I got from them. Because I wasn't one of them, but I stayed and worked with them as I promised.

At a minimum, it showed how much I appreciated what they did and that I was willing to do it too. The money we raised for our collective event made it cheaper for them to bring their spouses and partners.

I remember crawling into bed after the night shift ended, so exhausted, and I slept for about twelve hours.

The tertiary effect of all of these things was that even more people wanted to come to join our squadron. We could cherry-pick the best mechanics, the best sailors, because all of a sudden, we were the number one unit. All because we cared about people and worked to show them we valued them. It bled into everything we did.

While leading the 250 Sailors of VFA-83, the unit was awarded the 2009 Commander Naval Air Forces Aviation Battle Effectiveness Award. The Battle Effectiveness Award criterion is the command's overall readiness to carry out its assigned wartime tasks and is based on a year-long evaluation. The competition for the award is, and has always been, extremely keen. To win, a ship or unit must demonstrate the highest battle readiness.

We also won the CAPT Michael J. Estocin Award as the Navy's Strike Fighter Squadron of the Year, and the 2010 CNO Safety Award.

The last one was one of the most important to me. How did we do it? Well, anyone who has been in the military knows that alcohol-related incidents can be a big deal, even fatal at times. When units are between deployments is often when this kind of thing happens. Knowing this, I set a standard for our unit.

I stood in front of them and said, "Hey, look, I know you are going to go out and drink and probably party like crazy."

Some of those gathered laughed.

"I will pay for any cab fare rather than see you drive intoxicated. On any night you need cab fare back to your residence because you're drinking, it will be free to you."

Some of the sailors looked at each other as if to ask if I was being serious.

In response, I told them I was, indeed, serious. "All you have to do is just bring me the receipt, walk into my office, I'm going to cut you a check, or I'm going to hand you cash. That's it. We're done. No questions."

"Yeah, right," I heard the comments. "You know, he's gonna want to know if you're drinking, and you could get into trouble for it."

But one kid named Tony, one of the ones I had worked with side by side on the deck of the carrier, walked in one Monday morning and tossed down a $35 cab receipt as if to see if I would actually follow through with what I had told them.

I turned to my XO. "Call quarters," I said. "I want everybody in the hangar bay in 10 minutes."

As soon as everybody arrived, I walked out with Tony by my side.

"Hey, everybody, I know you're working really hard. I just wanted to take a moment because I want you to know how serious I am about this drunk driving thing. And how important it is to me." I handed the mic to Tony and said, "Hey, Tony, go tell everyone what just happened."

"I was drinking this weekend," he told them. "I took a cab home. This morning, I walked in, gave the Skipper the receipt for $35, and he paid for it."

"Thanks, Tony," I said. "I'm here because I want everybody to give him a round of applause for doing the right thing. He was drinking. He knew it. He got a cab. He's safe. That was the best 35 bucks I've ever spent."

Everybody gave him a round of applause, all 250 people, and off they went. The incident solidified how important it was for them to come to me if anything happened because I cared about people first.

It wasn't all just about awards. We wrote articles to improve safety within the F/A-18 community, and we crushed it. All because of our attention to detail. It was picking trash up off the floor and valuing people, and holding them to a higher standard. Everything that I had learned in the Blue Angels and with Admiral Keating, I got to put into practice. And it worked. And it works in any organization that wants to be the best.

For sailors, that meant I had to make sure that they had an environment that was safe, physically and mentally, and often when I talk about that, I use that bathroom example. To me, it's so much more than just fixing the toilets to be functional. It proved to be so much more meaningful to the members of our squadron than that.

Basically, I knew the unit that I wanted to be a part of. So I worked to create the environment I wanted to work in and that others did too. When I talk to companies, I often tell them if you set the bar low, then that's exactly what everybody will achieve. And if you set it high, that's what most people will achieve. There may be one or two who don't, but it's okay to identify them. But if we set the bar high, people will achieve that level of excellence. They truly will. In fact, most people want discipline and standards, and they truly desire to be the best. I know the sailors in my unit did.

But no story of a military career would be complete without a couple of war stories. We all have them, and here are a couple of mine.

19

SQUIRTERS

Our squadron was stationed on the *USS Eisenhower* in 2009 and 2010. We were still engaging the enemy in Afghanistan at a pretty high level at that time. In 2009, we flew a lot of missions and then rotated home for four months. After that, we went back for another seven-month deployment. Essentially, we were away from home for 13 out of 17 months.

But we were operational, and that's what we trained for. For many of us, this type of mission, to engage the enemy, was the very reason we joined the military.

During that time, we flew a couple of interesting missions, not that any of them were overly dull, but as pilots, we would call them "routine."

However, a few of them were pretty exciting. On one of those missions, there were some special forces operators we knew were out of Little Creek. That meant they were Navy

Seals, but we didn't know exactly who they were or what their mission was.

As we are flying in, we were talking to the guys on the ground through a secure channel. We had to descend into a valley, and we had some cloud cover. As a result, we were on instruments, using our ground radar system to descend in a spiral even though we couldn't always see clearly.

Anytime that you're supporting ground forces, you work in pairs. So we had two F/A-18s, a pair consisting of myself and George "Simple Jack" Wilkening. I was the flight lead since Simple Jack was pretty new. We flew in what was called a low stack, one of us at a higher elevation than the other. Since you always want to keep a forward-looking system on the bad guys, or the position where you believe they are, as you're trying to identify them, we were in a counter-rotating orbit across the circle from each other.

We were a little bit low and underneath a cloud layer. At the same time, I was talking to the special forces operators on the ground and a joint tactical controller specifically, trying to figure out exactly what we needed to do and how we could help.

The longer we stayed, the lower we got on gas. So we coordinated a tanker to come meet us, so we wouldn't have to break off and fly to them, leaving the ground forces exposed and without air support.

"Look, Simple Jack, why don't you leave, go get gas, and I'll stay here?"

This is what we call yo-yo operations, where one fighter stays down to protect while the other refuels, and then we reverse roles. The other fighter goes up to the tanker, so you both stay full and ready. Simple Jack goes up, and things are starting to heat up on the ground. But it was taking a long time, and I was starting to get low on gas. We were getting pretty close to employing against the enemy.

"Hey, how much time do you think you need to go get gas?" the Joint Tactical Air Controller (JTAC) asked.

"Maybe 10 minutes at the most," I told him.

"Okay, go now."

Our aircraft were equipped with technology that allowed us to see other aircraft and their positions digitally without the use of radar.

Oh man, I thought. I need to get gas and return right away.

I wasn't sure where Simple Jack was or how much time he had left to gather fuel. So I selected full afterburner, climbing up through the clouds, and rendezvoused with the tanker. And because I did a lot of airborne rendevous with the Blue Angels, I got pretty good at it. I went raging to join the KC-135 tanker and refueled. Simple Jack was still trying to rendezvous.

When I discovered this, I radioed him. "Hey, Simple Jack, I'm already on the tanker and ahead of you. I'm going back down as soon as I am full. Call me when you're on your way back in."

As soon as I was clear, I just split-sed back into the valley and was ready to engage. I don't think I was gone more than eight minutes.

I popped through the clouds and into the valley, and I

checked in with Overwatch. The JTAC cleared me to employ, so I destroyed the building, which blew up spectacularly.

Turned out we ended up destroying a weapons cache that was buried underneath and took out a handful of enemy combatants who were there, operating it.

Now when you blow up a building, naturally, those enemy soldiers who survived the blast would exit the building and run for it. When they did, we called them squirters. This is because they "squirt" out of the buildings and into the open. In this case, I could see them from my position up above

"Hey, I've got the squirters in sight," I said. "Just tell me to reengage, and I can neutralize them with 20 mike mike." That's what we call our 20-millimeter vulcan cannon machine gun employements.

"No, no, no, I got them," he told me. "They're mine."

"No problem," I said. "I mean, I can see them right now. I'm clear to roll in. I can employ within seconds."

"No, I got them. I'm going to take them out."

"Are you sure?" I asked. "Because I'm here. I'm ready."

We went back and forth, debating on who gets to neutralize the squirters from the building. He ended up taking them all out.

When the operation concluded, we had a very quick radio conversation. He told me he was from somewhere on the East Coast. And our squadron was also based on the East Coast, and while he didn't share details, he knew we were Navy, and we knew they were Navy, too.

You never said what unit you were a part of over open

comms. You never mentioned names. But it was pretty fun to work with somebody who was local in that regard.

I just remember laughing with him because we were both trying to neutralize the enemy. It was a great moment during one of the most memorable missions we flew over there.

But it wasn't the only one.

NINE LINE

CAS (Close Air Support) Nine Line Information:

Line 1 - Initial Point

This identifies the starting location from where the JTAC directs the aircraft to begin their attack. It can be either:

IP / Waypoint by name: "AMY"

Hasty IP, if the JTAC needs to create a new IP on the spot he will issue MGRS coordinates for the aircrew to create a new waypoint: "Hasty IP, Kilo Mike two-two-three-four."

Overhead, attacks may be conducted from an orbit of the target which allows aircrew to maintain eyes on the ground: "From the overhead"

Line 2 - Heading from IP to fly to the target: "two two zero - right"

The JTAC may direct a left or right offset to avoid a

known hazard, such as friendly artillery fire. The aircrew would stay on that side of the heading line when inbound to the target.

Line 3 - Distance from the IP to the target in km and should be accurate to a tenth of a km: "Nine point one"

Line 4 - Target Elevation given in feet above Mean Sea Level.

Read as sequential digits with the word "feet" after the digits: "Two three zero feet"

If lines 1-3 were abbreviated, the elevation transmission should begin with: "Elevation two three zero feet"

Line 5 - Target Description should be specific enough for the aircrew to recognize the target. Plain language. Concise but descriptive: "T-55"

Line 6 - Target Location.

100,000-meter square zone ID and numerical location digits.

There should be a noticeable pause between the easting and northing when reading MGRS grids so as to maintain an expected cadence.

"Kilo Mike seven eight one ... seven zero four"

Line 7 - Type of Mark the JTAC will use (talk-on, smoke, laser, or infrared) to mark the target: "Talk-on"

If using a laser, the JTAC will also pass the code he will use.

Line 8 - Friendlies Location from the target is given in meters and cardinal direction from the target: "friendlies west three five zero"

Line 9 - Egress: "Egress West, left pull to CHLOE"

Remarks

The following information should be included if applicable:

Laser-to-target line (LTL) (in degrees).

Desired type/number of ordnance and/or weapons effects.

Threat, location, and type of suppression (if any).

Any active Gun Target Line (GTL).

Hazards to aviation.

Weather.

Additional target information.

Night vision capability.

Other time considerations.

Friendly mark (if any).

Restrictions

The following information are restrictions and should always be read back.

Final attack heading.

Airspace Coordination Areas.

Danger close (if applicable and with commander's initials).

Time On Target / Time To Target.

9-line Readbacks

Lines 4, 6, and any restrictions are mandatory readback items.

--Taken from Naval SOP, 2021

T hings got a little exciting on another mission I flew with Simple Jack. People started giving us a hard time because every time Simple Jack and I flew together, we would generally employ. Keep in mind this was during General McChrystal's tightening of the rules of engagement, so we actually employed weapons less frequently.

McChrystal's tactical directive involved us trying to win the hearts and minds of the people of Afghanistan, so the use of weapons dropped off considerably.

On this particular mission, Simple Jack and I were out and orbiting in what we call a Kill Box.

To explain this as simply as possible, the whole world is split up into a grid system. If you're flying general support and the Navy didn't have something specific for you, they would send you to a box where you would orbit. If something happened or they needed you somewhere, they would deploy you from that location and direct you to the position where you were needed.

While we orbited in this box, we got an immediate call to support a TIC, Troops In Contact notice. We got an initial vector, and we're told to Buster, which means get to this location as fast as possible because friendly forces are engaged with the enemy, and bullets are flying.

We followed orders and flew to the area as fast as possible. When we arrived, we contacted the JTAC on the ground. While we were talking to them, we could hear the machine gunfire in the background over the radio.

Normally, you would check in when you arrived on the scene and ask questions like, "How's it going? What's the situation like?" This time, they went straight into a nine-line brief.

"Standby for nine-line," he said, and immediately we recieved the information described at the beginning of this chapter. We told them what ordinance we had and what we could employ as needed.

The troops were pinned down between two hills in a valley, a north and south ridge line. As we were running in, we'd been cleared to engage upon arrival. This meant the troops below were in big trouble. I took the north ridge line, and Simple Jack took the south.

We employed on those positions and shocked the enemy a little bit with our quick bombing run. We both dropped the two bombs we had with us. The only weapon we had left was the 500 rounds of 20 mike mike we each carried.

"Hey, the enemy is emplaced on the ridge above us," the controller said. "They're shooting down at us, so we need you to deploy some machine gun fire on this ridgeline."

Dusk had arrived, and we were a little bit low on gas, but there was no way we could leave these troops engaged and not help them out by neutralizing this threat. Essentially they were pinned down. We're not going to leave until we absolutely have to, because we're in the fight with them now.

Under normal circumstances, when you run in on a ridgeline, and you're going to pull the trigger on the machine gun, you want to run parallel with the ridge line because you want to shoot in line with the longitudinal axis of the plane and the ridge.

Instead, when the call came, the JTAC gave me a run-in heading perpendicular to the ridge line. "That's not gonna work," I told him. "I need to come in along the ridge line."

"You can't. There's a Dutch helicopter coming in, and they're gonna fire rockets along that vector. We already gave them that heading."

Well, I could only come in the way that he cleared me to come in. Otherwise, I could end up taking out the Dutch helicopter.

So Simple Jack and I separate so we are 180 degrees across from each other as we orbit overhead. We can employ an overlapping field of fire. I wasn't cleared in yet, but I orbited in a position where I could roll in as soon as I was cleared hot.

The Dutch helicopter came in, "Whoosh, whoosh, whoosh," and hosed off a bunch of rockets at the ridgeline, and then I got cleared.

By now, it is full dusk, and I am flying perpendicular, essentially straight at the mountain ridge. And as I'm rolling in, I would normally come in on a 15-degree dive when using the Vulcan Cannon on an F/A-18. It can fire 6000 rounds a minute, but you only trigger two-second bursts because you don't want to overheat the barrel of the gun. If you do, it can melt.

Even two seconds is a lot of bullets, and it's longer than you think when you're flying in fast and pulling the trigger at the same time. As I'm rolling in on my dive because it was dusk, I could see the enemy positions along the ridgeline due to the sparkle and tracer fire from the machine guns pointed down at our guys in the valley.

"Holy cow," I said. I can see them plain as day. But I'm

coming in toward the ridgeline at a tough angle, and really, I need to fire horizontally.

Well, I only knew one way to get the bullets from side to side, starting from the center, moving to the left, and then sweeping back across the ridge to the right to get the maximum effect without changing my vector. And that's kicking the rudder.

So I did. As I fired, I used the rudder, spraying the ridgeline from side to side. As I popped off and came up for another attack, I heard the JTAC on the ground.

"That was awesome!" he said. "Can you do that again?"

So I pitched back up and to the left. The Dutch helicopter came back around and shot a bunch of rockets again. Once they finished and I was cleared back in, I dove and again kicked the rudder and strafed the entire ridge, enemy muzzle flashes and tracer rounds guiding my aim before I pitched up and off.

In those two passes. I sent 500 rounds of 20 Mike Mike High Explosive rounds into the side of that hill. Those types of rounds explode on contact, taking out more than one enemy at a time. Between the two of us, we saved all of the coalition forces on the ground. I don't know how many enemy combatants were eliminated, but a lot of them. It was one of the greatest moments I had in combat.

We flew back to the ship, and we went in to debrief the mission. When I showed the video, some of the Top Gun graduates said, "What was that?"

"That was the only way that I knew how to get the bullets over where I needed them to be."

We were never trained to do that. We trained to bomb. Or to get a cluster of high explosive impact rounds of 20 Mike Mike in one spot. Or you will do what you call a John Wayne, where you strafe over the enemy lengthwise, like the vector I wanted but that the Dutch helicopter had. You'd never request a horizontal employment.

"What made you think of that?" they asked me in the debrief.

I thought about it, and the truth was, just like in other things, I'm just I'm not afraid to fail.

I knew where I needed the bullets. And I knew there was only one way to get the bullets there. So that's what I tried.

And if it hadn't worked, I would have tried something else.

Following that particular mission, the Chief of Naval Operations put me in for the American Legion Valor Award. It's something they give to one person in the Air Force, one in the Army, one Marine, and one Navy person each year. That year, I won it for the Navy.

Here's the funny thing about that award. There's an order of precedence of ribbons and medals you receive when you are in the military. This relates to where they go on your dress uniform. The American Legion Valor Award is not in the normal precedents or order of awards. So it's in a drawer upstairs at my house, because I never knew where to put it.

It was nice to be recognized, but what was much more important to me is that we saved all coalition lives, and the enemy took a beating that day. I didn't need to get any kind of award for it. I just needed to know that those troops, the good guys, were okay.

My wife went to receive that award in 2010 for me because I was still deployed at the time.

In 2010, we were super limited in the way we conducted combat missions in Afghanistan because of the policy shift to the hearts and minds mentality, which in my opinion, was not a great way to fight a war.

But the strategy was not up to me. I simply did the best I could to take care of the people around me. And that led me to even more great places in my career.

LEADERSHIP AND THE F-35

Being in military leadership is tough. You want to be connected with your people and support them, but much like Admiral Keating and his Diet Coke with Lime, those who serve with you often misinterpret your orders or exactly what you mean when you say something. This is in part due to your rank or position. You are in charge, and you want them to take orders seriously. But they often misunderstand your passion to make their jobs easier.

I learned from Admiral Keating to value the words "we" and "our." It wasn't my squadron or my mission, but our squadron and our mission.

I tried encouraging those around me to see things the same way, but it did not always work perfectly.

For example, we were in Virginia Beach just after our 2010 Afghanistan deployment. One of the junior officers was standing squadron duty officer, and I was supposed to do a functional check flight. Maintenance was having some problems getting the aircraft ready.

I went to the Squadron Duty Officer, Ryan "iLean" Anderson, who basically got his call sign because he had a little bit of a lean in his shoulders.

"Hey, do me a favor iLean," I said. "Call down to maintenance and tell them that I am available at their convenience for that check ride."

"No problem, Skipper," he said.

While I was standing there, he picked up the phone and said, "Hey, the Skipper wants to know if that jet is ready for his check ride."

I said, "iLean, tell them to hold on and that you will call them back."

He hung up and just looked at me.

"What you told them just now is not what I said," I told him. "What I said was I am available at their convenience. And that when they're ready, I, too, will be ready. You called them and told them to get that airplane ready now because the Skipper is ready. That's a totally different message."

"I understand," he told me. "I apologize."

"So call them back. Tell them that I am in no rush. I have all afternoon. They have plenty of time to fix the issue correctly. And when it's available, I will execute the functional check flight."

"Yes, sir."

"And I'll stand right here while you make that call."

And I did.

As the Commander, you had to be careful to make it

really clear what you meant and make sure that got communicated without the recipient adding their own filter or level of urgency. For me, it was more important that the people who were fixing the aircraft felt comfortable and got it right than that they conform to any imaginary timeline.

But iLean didn't hear me that way. So I had to correct it.

There are other important aspects to leadership as well. I wanted to make myself super accessible, but I also tended to be decisive. Part of being a fighter pilot is the ability to look at choices, make evaluations quickly and make good decisions in a short period of time.

But as you move up to command positions, you need to rely on the perceptions of others. And every time I briefed a new Department Head, the middle management of the Navy, or even the Chiefs or anybody that reported to me, I would say this:

"Look, you may come in with a great idea. And I encourage you to do so. I may give you an answer that you disagree with. And you might walk out of the office, down the hallway, and you'll stew on it. You might think maybe you didn't sell it right, or you wish you would have said something different.

"If that's the case, come back in and reengage because maybe you didn't sell it right. Maybe you didn't tell me all the information that I needed to make a sound decision. Maybe I didn't explain all the details of why I made that decision. We'll sit down, and I'll listen to you explain, perhaps better than you did the first time.

I'll share why I made the decision and why I think it's in

our squadron's or people's best interest. But please do try again. But once that decision is made, don't return a third time. Once we have finished our second discussion, that should be sufficient.

The truth is, they were often right. My job was to train people to be good at their jobs and to be better leaders.

They might pair a couple of pilots together. One of them might be Junior, who might not have the right qualifications.

"What are you doing?" I would ask. "Why did you change this? We put a lot of time into those schedules."

They might leave, but then they would come back and explain: this is why we made this change. This is why we're adding this additional responsibility to this junior officer's duties. This is why we're recommending that they fly with this person.

My perception of them might differ from the professional reality and how they interacted with others in the squadron. If anyone came back a second time from an operational or maintenance process perspective and they believed in whatever they might be trying to do, I would say, "Okay, if you believe in it that much, and you accept responsibility and accountability for it, go forth, and execute your plan."

I had learned alot and was on the fast track, headed toward the highest levels of Naval command. To recap, this had been my naval career up to that point.

I started by going to flight school while Lisa and I were still dating, in a long-distance relationship. After we were married, we moved fourteen times over the next 22 years. As soon as we tied the knot in California, we moved immediately to Kingsville, Texas.

From there, we went to Jacksonville for F/A-18 operational training.

Then we moved to Japan, where our first son was born.

After that, we moved back to the States and El Toro, near Los Angeles, then San Diego, where our second son was born.

While I was with the Blue Angels, we moved to Pensacola, Florida, where we stayed for three years,

Then we moved to Virginia Beach, and I deployed twice to Iraq from there.

Moving to Colorado and Hawaii followed that as the Aide de Camp to Admiral Keating.

Then we moved back to Virginia Beach for my command tour, which included two deployments to Afghanistan.

Then came my Pentagon tour. The Pentagon is a tough place to work, and I got to see the inside of the Navy administration and all our struggles with the F-35 program. Mistakes were made, the program took longer than it should have, and at times it was even frustrating.

I was tasked with becoming the Navy's first Commanding Officer of the only stealth squadron in the US Navy at that time, Strike Fighter Squadron ONE ZERO ONE, based in Elgin Air Force Base, Florida.

It was the next step in my Navy career. The next step would be major command at the highest levels in the Navy.

But my life had changed and was changing. And I had a

huge decision to make, one that involved both my family and my career.

So at that point, due to many different factors, I decided to retire. But to fully explain that, I need to back up just a little bit.

FULL THROTTLE, CHANGE IN DIRECTION

You have to understand I was fully, totally, 100% committed to the Navy. Not that all my superiors were perfect or that there were no people I didn't want to work for or with. Retirement really was not about that.

I love the Navy. I love the camaraderie. I love the internal organization of naval aviation, even when some of those people have cringed at the changes the Navy and the military have made. Some I like, some I don't, but they didn't play a factor in my decision to leave.

In reality, when you have landed on an aircraft carrier in a strike fighter airplane, you are in a different club, and anyone in that club has tremendous respect and admiration for others in the club. There is extreme respect for the teams and the other personnel that keep the aircraft flying, keep the ship operational, and work to keep others around you safe.

In the fighter pilot community, many of us have similar personality types. We've got the same fighting spirit. I loved being a part of all of it, and I didn't have a strong desire to leave.

But I had to make a really difficult decision. The kids were in high school. They were involved in sports and clubs, had friends, and were developing roots. But we knew we would not be in one place for long.

I was planning to screen for major command, and I assumed, based on my flying, my fit reps, and my understanding of the system from working for Admiral Keating and others, that I would do well and excel in that area of my career. The next step would be an Air Wing Commander.

That meant there were more moves in our future. That was promising from a Naval professional standpoint if I intended to continue to build my career and someday retire at the highest level possible.

But I had to think of Lisa and the kids and the toll my career had already taken on them. On top of all the moves, in my tour in Japan, the first three years in an operational squadron, I was gone eight out of 12 months. That was just the operational tempo of the forward-deployed squadron.

After that, I worked as an instructor, and I was gone on a lot of weekends trying to build up flight time because I wanted to become a Blue Angel, and frankly, that's what it took.

But when I got selected for the Blues, that meant I was gone 35 weekends a year plus 14 weeks during the winter for training. I did that for three years. When I went to my

Department Head tour, I went straight into deployment. We were gone for three months during Shock and Awe, and then I was home for a year, which was really kind of the first year that I was home with any regularity.

But following that brief break (the timeframe in which I did the Iron Man), I deployed again in 2005. After that, I joined Admiral Keating and was away from home for over sixty trips. I made T-shirts similar to rock band tour shirts when I left his command as a tribute to how much we traveled together. It included the cities and the dates, like a Metallica tour. Those were times when I was not home with my family.

From there, I went straight to command and was gone to Afghanistan twice, once in 2009 and again in 2010. Then I was what we call a geographical bachelor at the Pentagon, running the F-35 program for a month until the kids got out of school and my family could come and join me.

After that, we moved on to Eglin Air Force Base while I stood up the first F-35 program. And granted, I wasn't gone as much while we were based there.

But we had this conversation a lot, and it got to the point where I felt like I could be a great dad or a great military leader, but it would be exceptionally hard to be really great at both. Honestly, at that point, I felt like I was an average to slightly above-average dad and a really great military leader, just based on the awards and recognition that the unit I led had received in the latter area. Those and the job opportunities I had showed excellence in my career.

Each one of those job opportunities moved me forward

toward more promotions, more military experience and accolades, and more responsibility. Still, they also came with more moves and more time away from home.

My son Wyatt was 15. He had his first girlfriend. But Lisa and I didn't really like Fort Walton Beach. We enjoyed the military people just fine, but to be honest, the racism in high school and in the community was just disgusting. Reprehensible. Kids were flying Confederate flags in their trucks on the way to school. The education that they were receiving was average at best and poor at worst.

That's not to discount the teachers or the school district there. But it just wasn't as good as what we had seen in Colorado, Virginia Beach, and other places where we lived.

And so, as the kids were in junior high and prepping for high school, we decided it was probably time to get out of the Navy.

And it was hard. Wyatt had to leave his girlfriend, who he truly cared about, in that high school infatuation way. I'll even say he loved his girlfriend. The boys had moved to nine different schools throughout their education. I don't know that Nick had ever attended two years in a row at the same school. He was just yearning for a group of steady friends.

We knew that we would retire to Colorado Springs someday, but we didn't know what that would look like until we made that decision.

And we did it kind of on a whim, to be perfectly honest, not really sure what we were going to do next. We knew we would have a military retirement income and that perhaps I had some capabilities that might provide income for us in the future.

It was tough on all of us, especially Lisa. There were a lot of tears.

From Wyatt, there were questions like "Can't we just stay?" and things like that. It wasn't so much my job that bothered him, but having to move again.

And to be honest, I kind of wanted to stay. I could have gotten a pretty senior job at Lockheed Martin in the F-35 program and moved up in that company quickly.

But that didn't negate the reasons we wanted to leave. The community was filled with racism and disrespect, and we just didn't want to raise our kids there. We wanted better schools for them, which was a huge factor in our decision to move.

So we started making plans.

Lisa started looking at houses in Colorado Springs but from our home in Florida. Remember, this was 2011-2012, and we had just gone through the housing bubble bursting . But she found a place she liked and was hot for this house. Excited might be the best word.

One day, I was in the kitchen, and Lisa came in and said, "Hey, that house that I've been looking at? They dropped the price by 50,000!"

"Well, fly out there tomorrow as soon as you can and go look at it."

"You know last-minute tickets are four hundred bucks?" she asked.

"Yeah, compared to the price of the house, that's nothing.

And we don't want to miss it," I told her. "But you gotta look at a couple of other houses, just for comparison and to be sure."

"No," she said. "This is the house."

She left the next morning and met a realtor who was also one of her girlfriends in Colorado Springs.

The phone rang before dinner that night.

"How was it?" I asked.

"We put a contract in on it," she told me.

Now we knew we were moving to Colorado Springs for sure.

Some of the reasons I accepted the house she wanted so easily was she had sacrificed so long in a supportive role so that I could pursue my dreams that I was thrilled to give back to her. I wanted her to have what she needed and what she wanted. It wasn't that I owed it to her or anything, but that she deserved my support in return for everything she enabled me to do.

Retiring and moving were both brutal decisions but absolutely the best ones we could have made at the time.

Where Lisa and I are now in our marriage, in our parenting, and in our professional careers, we would not change a thing.

23

THROTTLING BACK TO CIVILIAN LIFE

W hen I first left the Navy, I thought I would probably fly for FedEx. There are a lot of former Blue Angels, Navy pilots, and even Air Force flyers who work for them. They have good, regular routes, and you are home on a regular basis.

But instead, I started working for a company called Afterburner. Matt "Whiz" Buckley, a very dear friend of mine, who I went through flight training and instruction with, was working for them on the side.

The owner is Jim Murphy, just an incredible, ambitious, and innovative leader and the founder of the company.

Essentially the company is made up of elite military aviators and special operations personnel. The idea is to connect corporate strategy to execution with training programs that include keynotes, team-building seminars, workshops, training, coaching, and consulting programs that incorporate the culture of excellence we all learned at the highest levels of military performance.

I knew I had the ability to speak in front of others and teach. From the Blues and the units I led, I knew that the principles I used there enabled those organizations to achieve excellence.

And, of course, I have carried that forward in everything I have done since. This is where it all started.

"You should give this a shot, Intake," he told me.

The job would enable me to live where I wanted and travel as needed to give these talks, so it would work for me and my family.

So I applied, using him as a recommendation, and got the job. I started near the end of 2012 and worked there through most of 2014. During that time, I spoke with well over 100 companies, It was really good for me and my development as a speaker and an instructor, and I learned a lot about how to communicate my skills and knowledge to others.

While that covered the job part of things, at least for a while, I had to adjust to other things that, while others might think are simple, can be real challenges for anyone who has left the military and rejoined the civilian workforce.

I joked with my wife, Lisa. "I don't know how to make friends," I told her. "I haven't had to do that since college."

In the military community, you just show up at a squadron, and they throw a party for you. It's called a hail and farewell, and it's where you say goodbye to those people who are leaving and hello to the newcomers. You get to know a new set of faces, your wife gets involved in a new community of spouses, and your kids go to a new school with other kids who are in the same situation they are in. "Friends" are built in, and often you already know some of those who are leaving and some of those joining you on your new assignment.

Some of those friends last a lifetime. Some you see over and over throughout your career. Others kind of come and go with your orders: you are friends, or rather acquaintances for a few years when you work together, and then you both move on.

But the fighter pilot community is small, and you kind of end up a part of it by default. The Pacific fleet is its own community, and so are the Atlantic fleet and the squadrons on the east coast. The Blue Angels are a community all their own. Since I was in both the Pacific and the Atlantic fleets and worked at a high level, I had a large circle of military friends, and I still do.

For 22 years, all I would do was show up and poof, instant friends, which was really true. It was only partially true for Lisa because the Wives Club is a little different but similar in the way it works. Usually, the community was very welcoming for the boys, but if there were not as many kids who were the same age in the same unit, they were thrown to the wolves at whatever school they were in to make new friends, often knowing we would not be in the area long.

When it came to that, Wyatt was exceptional at making friends. That's just his outgoing personality. Nick had some challenges from time to time, and it was hard on him. The hardest was when we moved at the end of his fifth-grade year.

The school he attended in Virginia Beach started junior high in sixth grade, making it three years, sixth, seventh, and eighth grade. But we moved to Washington D.C. that summer, and he thought he was headed to junior high and suddenly found himself back in elementary school. That was devastating for him, and he really struggled with that transition.

So when we moved to Colorado Springs, I still traveled extensively with Afterburner. That was mostly during the week when corporations were working, training, and looking for keynote speakers and workshops.

Lisa, being the amazing support and operations logistics person that she is, got the boys in school and got them all set up in swimming, which was their sport of choice. Nick eventually ended up running cross country, and in doing so, he finally found this remarkable friend group that was really supportive. Our boys tapped roots in Colorado Springs with their high school friends that remain very deep even as they have moved on to the Naval Academy and forward in their own careers.

The Afterburner work was incredible. I went to Thailand to give a speech to Macquarie International overseas with Matt Buckley, the guy that got me hired in the first place. Even though I was gone a lot during the week, Lisa and I made some really wonderful friends, including parents involved in the swim team.

But Lisa was much better at it than I am. I would get my

fill of military guys and that camaraderie when I was on the road and at an Afterburner event. Then sometimes, when I got home, I would just need to turn the light switch off, be quiet, and recharge my social batteries.

But the transition was also hard because I missed the leadership. I watched many of my friends and peers continue to promote to higher ranks and greater elements of responsibility in the Navy. So even though I had Afterburner and I had some friends, I struggled with missing those I knew in the military.

In reality, I had to find my footing again and rebuild my professional reputation on the civilian side. Because I was essentially starting from scratch. This is really common for those who leave the military. I mean, I can go into a job interview or a place and say, "I led an F/A-18 squadron in combat, and I stood up the Navy's first F-35C Squadron."

They would nod and smile because, certainly, that commands a lot of respect, but people respond by saying, "Yeah, that's great. But what do you know about logistics? Do you have your master's in business? What do you know about supply chain management? And what do you know about income statements and shareholder equity statements?"

Many of those things I knew about, but we might have called it something else in the military. I didn't have the right piece of paper or the civilian equivalent in education, and even my bachelor's degree was in an area I hadn't worked directly in for over two decades.

Afterburner not only taught me a lot about speaking and

teaching but showed me the reason to really lean in with that business aspect and increase my education. I hadn't given that much attention up to that point.

This is where the message that I try to send to corporate America when I speak. Somebody may have driven a tank or been an infantryman. That veteran may have worked in supply or administration, really any military field. Although your company may not drive tanks and may not carry rifles, these men and women come out of the military with exceptional skills that are easily transferable.

They're exceptionally adaptable and flexible, and they learn quickly. They understand teams, are loyal, and once they join your team, they are committed. Their whole entity and their reason for being are formed around the team and working for and with others. Take the chance; you'll be pleasantly surprised.

But for that to work, your company must have a common purpose, a goal, and a reason for employees to align with your mission.

The biggest challenge in corporate America nowadays is establishing a culture with a common purpose where everybody is working towards something they value, which aligns with the team's strategic vision. It's easy to say, but in reality, that's super hard to do.

No paycheck compares to that feeling of belonging. Either you empower your people and give them the freedom to both succeed and fail, or you take that away from them, and that leads to them feeling undervalued.

In turn, they give you exactly what they have to to keep

getting paid, but they will find their value and purpose when they leave work.

And if an opportunity comes along, they will leave for somewhere they feel empowered and that they belong.

When I left the military, I searched for that. I found some of it through Afterburner, but that wasn't my long-term answer.

So in 2014, I joined the team at United Airlines.

24

UNITED AND FINDING MY WAY

I struggled until I found my place at United. In 2015, I applied to be part of the leadership, excellence, and professionalism team, where we were going to basically do the professional keynote and inspirational type of speeches we did at Afterburner, but exclusively to the United pilot group.

We planned to travel to the pilot bases around the country, eventually reaching all 12,000 of those who flew for the company. There were about 30 of us on the team. As that position grew, I began to anchor in Colorado with United.

Part of the reason I went all in when it came to working for United was so that I could have the flexibility to execute a larger strategic financial plan.

In short, I went into real estate. Already, we owned several single-family rentals around the country we had acquired while I was in the military, but I wanted to delve into the multi-family housing market.

Through my work with United, I could do that, still keep flexibility, and fly with United on a part-time basis to keep my pilot qualifications current.

Through the leadership program and flying, I decided to apply for a management position with them. I decided I could either go all in on public speaking or all in on management, not both. I made the decision that management would be a better choice for my future. I started to climb the corporate ladder.

Around that same time, in 2017, United asked me to lead the team that put Fleet Week together. Obviously, I had a unique experience running air shows and an understanding of what that took. But that turned into a great opportunity for me.

Fleet Week led me to the Patriot Jet Team, which we will discuss in another chapter. I also connected with many professional business people in Colorado Springs, and I finally felt that I had found my civillian squadron. They became kind of a replacement for my military family, especially those on the Patriot Team.

So while I struggled for about five years, from 2012 to 2017, that experience helped me to find what I thought my career would look like. I became more involved with the United Training Center, which got me involved in even more projects. I built a new form of loyalty with my new groups of co-workers and friends, and they were the people I was excited to spend more time with.

My move to the United management team happened in 2019 , and it helped me to establish my name at the company. As mentioned, my reputation in the civilian world was different than my military reputation, and I felt like things were finally headed in the right direction on the civilian side.

But the beauty of being in my 50s (which I was at that point) and being successful was that I could make choices when circumstances changed, and pick the right path for me.

The position I took was a management grooming position: from there, I could become a senior manager. Once established there, I had a shot at becoming a Director and then a Managing Director. Of course, I had already been a Managing Director in the Navy. I understood I needed to cut my teeth and prove my worth at United before I could rise to that type of position again.

But then a guy got hired over me, and in my opinion, he did not belong in the job. He wasn't a people person and didn't have my life experience, just more tenure at United. And the thing that topped off the issues I had with him was really a simple one.

I was actually hired as the first flight manager in the Training Center as part of this idea of developing leadership continuity through a growth grooming program. But as the pandemic hit in 2020, there was a significant leadership change. Instead of a leadership grooming position, it became a mid-level supervisory position. That wasn't what I'd signed up for or what I really wanted to do.

The person who got hired ahead of me had an interesting

resume. He was a United Captain but hadn't done anything apart from that. I was a First Officer but had an incredible military background. But he got spot promoted partly because of his time with the company. In the airline world, if you have been a Captain rather than a First Officer, for some reason, having flown in the left seat makes you a better leader. But it just wasn't true.

I felt like I was overqualified for what I was doing and he was underqualified.

My senior manager asked me to write an email one day for him. Of course, that was no problem. I'd written a lot of emails on many subjects through the years.

But I wrote it based on my experience, which had been in the Training Center. I knew what the instructors needed to know to do their job and what they wanted to know. So that's how I crafted the email, giving them the information they would need and wanted. This was our introduction to them as their leaders, and I wanted to set the tone from the beginning.

But he changed it into this absolute junk email that had nothing substantial in it.

"You know, I made some changes to your draft. What do you think?" he asked.

After I read it over, I said, "Well, I think what you needed to convey and what I wrote in the email are the same." I then explained to him the reasons for what I wrote and why I thought those things were important to share. "I think you should send that email or at least something with all the information I provided you."

"I'm gonna send mine," he said, clearly unhappy with my response.

That afternoon on the drive home, I called Brian Quigley, my boss, and said, "Thanks for the opportunity, but I am not the guy you need in this position. You need a 30-year-old who needs to learn before he is ready to move up. I'm not your guy. I was doing this 20 years ago in the Navy."

"I understand," he said.

"Look, the job changed. Call me if you want me to be in a Director or Managing Director position. But otherwise, I'm out of the management game."

Fortunately, he knew me and accepted what I had to say at face value, not as a reflection on United or the team there.

"I'm all in for United, but this is not the job that I want to do or the job I was hired for," I told him.

Eventually, in 2021, they offered me the opportunity to apply for the position of Managing Director of Aviation Safety for United, and I competed competitively for that position. I got through three rounds of interviews, but after I went to Chicago for the final round, they let me know I didn't get that job.

That moment was an epiphany for me. If there was a single job at United that I would be most qualified for, that would be it. I was exceptionally suited to that role due to my military experience, aerial investigation and leadership, and it was right up my alley.

My skills totally matched up, and I was excited about it because I'm passionate about safety. But when they turned me down, it told me something.

To move up at United, you have to be all in United. And I was all in. But at that point, I recognized, "I'm not the leader they wanted."

I was okay with that. The commercial aviation world allowed me to pivot and go do the things I really wanted to do. United is a great company, and they've given me incredible opportunities. They're remarkably supportive. I just don't fit into their leadership styles and roles.

After the interview, I talked to my wife on the way home and said, "Hey, I didn't get the job.

"I'm so sorry to hear that," she said.

"No, actually, it is totally enlightening to me," I told her. "Because that was the job that I wanted. That was the job that my whole aviation career was driving towards, one that I was amply qualified for. And so I am officially off the corporate ladder."

"Once you get off the ladder, it's tough ever to get back on," she told me. And I knew it was true.

But the beauty of it is now I own my future. What has happened since is Maverick, the Blue Angels Foundation, the Patriots, and another movie adventure. That free time that United allows, that's just in the nature of being a commercial airline pilot, enables me to pursue opportunities.

I have pivoted into fulfilling my passion for fundraising to support the prevention of veteran suicide and doing things that I want to do and enjoy doing. So with no stress of trying to climb up a ladder that I just am not interested in doing, I've been able to do so much more.

Paramount has recognized my skill set, and the Blue

Angel Foundation has recognized it. Fortune 500 companies are hiring me to come to teach their executive leadership teams, recognizing my abilities in ways that United just doesn't. That liberation has opened up another world of opportunity.

For United, I still teach Human Factors and Pilot Development. I still do training for them, but now it's on my own schedule. And I still fly for them and maintain my commercial pilot status. I do that because I really enjoy doing it. I love integrating with line pilots. I love talking to them about mentorship, leadership command, and the physiological effects of flying. I believe in those things, so it's easy for me.

But that isn't my life; it isn't my career, and I've become the pilot of my own destiny. A part of that certainly started with Fleet Week and becoming a part of another team that changed my life in so many ways.

25

THE PATRIOTS

Taking charge of organizing Fleet Week for United satisfied another desire inside of me, and that was to be on the air show circuit again. Even though my time with the Blue Angels was incredibly intense, it was worth all the effort put into it. Having served as number7 pilot and the narrator my first year gave me a lot of insight into how things actually worked.

That time as the #7 for the Blues also allowed me to make connections that lasted a lifetime. That came into play during my first year running the show.

During Fleet Week, there is a family day event consisting of all the United maintainers and their families.

At that event, I bumped into a pilot named Scott "Banker" Ind, who was the number five pilot on the Blue Angels when I was number seven. He was now flying for the Patriots Jet

Team, a private aerial demonstration team based in California who were flying at the show.

"Hey, how are you?" he says.

"Great. Great to see you," I said. I hadn't seen him in 20 years.

"Good to see you. How's your wife? How're your kids?"

We did the usual small talk for about 20 seconds. "Hey, we're looking for a guy," he said. "Are you interested?"

"Yes, I'm interested," I told him. The prospect of flying in the show again truly excited me, but I didn't know for sure what that would look like.

"Okay, I will let them know."

"Talk to me about the team. What's it like?" I asked/

The hardest maneuver in a delta for the six-ship is a delta roll. It's hardest for the guys on the left wing. Because the guys on the right wing are pulling and adding power as they go around. And the guys on the inside are driving in and reducing power.

As a Blue Angel, it was the hardest maneuver that I had to learn, and it was the hardest to execute. It's really disorienting, and it's a challenge even for a great pilot.

After we talked about the team members, Dean "Wilbur" Wright #1, Rob "Stache" Hutchison #2, John "Bordz" Posson #3, Paul "Sticky" Strickland #4, and Jeff "Mojo" Jess #7 and who they were, and what it was like to fly with them, he said, "Hey, Intake, let me put it this way. We don't roll left and drink whiskey during the debriefs."

"That'll work," I said.

Two weeks later, I met Randy "Howler" Howell, the

owner of the team, along with another pilot, John "Bordz" Posson, at Bryon Airfield, where the team is based.

I jumped in the back of Howler's jet, an L-39, and we went out for a show practice. He flew the show profile, and I was just observing from the back seat.

"Hey, why don't you fly and take us back by show center?"

We were in a climbing left-hand turn, and to get back to show center would mean making a right turn in the opposite direction of this climb. And instead, I just executed a left 270, a really rapid U-turn in the sky, then headed back because it was faster.

"Oh, I didn't really expect that," Randy said.

"Well, I figured I'd just expedite it," I told him.

That was my debut with the Patriots.

As you might have gathered from my unconventional maneuver of kicking the rudder to strafe a ridgeline, I'm a little bit more of an artist in the air rather than a technician. I put the plane where it needs to be, and I kind of "feel" that.

Randy is exceptionally mechanical as a pilot in that if the maneuver calls for 30 degrees up and 50 degrees of angle bank, that is exactly how he executes it.

I don't know how to explain it other than that I just fly largely by instinct, putting the plane in the right space at the right time. So he could see that I could fly the plane, and I knew what I was doing.

After we landed, Randy said, "Good job. Let's go fly some formation. I'll put you in the front seat of this jet. "Bordz" our number 3 pilot, will be in the back seat.

First of all, I had no idea how to start this plane or taxi it either. I don't know the emergency procedures. And because this is a Czechoslovakian trainer, all the labels and instructions are in Czechoslovakian and use the metric system, unlike the Imperial system we use in the U.S.

He saw my confusion as I looked around, and said, "Yeah, that's no big deal. Let me give you a quick rundown."

As I'm strapping in, he stands up next to me. I haven't been in a jet for five years at this point, except for the flight I just did with him, where I was in the back seat.

He gave me a quick set of instructions: "Hit those buttons, which will introduce the air into the jet engine. Watch this. Move the throttle around, and then go click, click, click," he flipped three switches, and I watched carefully. "Then, when you're ready, we'll taxi out."

" Okay. Sure," I said, getting the feel for the aircraft pretty quickly.

We got started up, and Bordz was in the back seat. We taxied out, which was pretty easy for me. We executed a formation takeoff, which went fine. There was just a lot going on as I got used to taking off in a different airplane, but everything worked.

Once airborne, he said, "Hey, we're just going to do some maneuvers. We'll try some stuff and see how it goes."

"Sure," I said. So we did a few pretty simple maneuvers, and it's going okay. I got a better feel for the aircraft the longer I flew it.

"All right, you know, you seem to be doing all right. You want to do a loop?"

"Yeah, of course, I'll do a loop," I said.

The Blue Angels, when they start a loop, they say, "up we go." "Up we" is the preparatory call. Then we said a protracted "go." On the 'G,' you started pulling, and you all stopped at the end of the 'O.'

But the Patriots use a little bit more Thunderbird-like verbiage because there were Thunderbirds on the team, and they were the ones who developed the calls. Before the command, they give the airspeed, 650, and then say pitching now, and the pitching is the preparatory command, and the now is when you pull. And so that now was way more aggressive than what I'd been used to. And so Howler said, "Pitching now."

He pulled, and right away, I found myself behind. I tried to catch up and rejoin on the upside of this loop. I kept fighting the aircraft and ended up rendezvousing at the top of the loop, inverted. I was able to get back into formation and finish it as a part of the formation. We did some other meneuvers after that, but I don't remember what it was. It all went pretty smoothly.

Once we got back and landed, I could hear Bordz talking with Randy about how things had gone.

Once we were back in the hangar, Randy said, "Hey, we want to offer you the job."

"Fantastic," I said. "I'm excited about the opportunity. Of course, I have to call my wife and talk to her about it. Can I call you back this afternoon with a decision?"

At this point, I had to drive back to Sacramento Airport to fly back home. That's when Bordz spoke up and said, "I've never seen anybody rendezvous, inverted, at the top of a loop."

"Well, to tell you the truth, I was kind of pissed that he lost me at the beginning. It was, you know, good to keep fighting the maneuver," I told him. But in part, I probably owe my persistence in that maneuver to getting me the job with the team.

I called Lisa from Sacramento airport. " Hey, look, they offered me the job."

I wanted to make sure I had her support because the airshows would once again be stressful for the family. They can consume a lot of your weekend time, and it's a relatively high-risk activity.

"That's great," she said.

"What do you think?" I waited for her answer.

"Well, it's not really what I think. What do you think?"

"Lisa, it made me feel alive. And I really want to do it."

"I think you should do it then," she said.

There are two great points in that, in that very simple communication between Lisa and I. One, when I said it made me feel alive, it, it was re-energizing. For me, it was more than the intensity of the flight itself. It was the belonging, the group, the adrenaline rush. And the re-engagement with life, if you will, rather than the humdrum of work.

Second, her asking, "What do you want to do?" When I told her, she said, "Well, I think you should do it," she again showed what her chosen role has been the whole time, which is total support of me and our family. That really short exchange encompasses our marriage, which is really wonderful.

Of course, I had to get type qualified before I could fly in shows, which meant getting certified on that airplane. I did that in November 2017. I went out, flew, and got the certification I needed to fly the L-39. We held some practices after that.

My first show as part of the team came in March of 2018, down in Yuma, Arizona. It was during spring break. The boys were at the Naval Academy and would be home, but this show would be happening during the same week.

One of the things that Randy told me when I started was once you commit to the team, I need your full commitment because we do six or seven shows a year, and they pay a lot of money for us to show up. It pays a lot less if there are five airplanes instead of six. So I need to know that you're in.

"I'm in. I get it," I said. This related to my mode throughout my career: a commitment to the unit no matter what.

Right off the bat, that got tested with the boys coming up for spring break. I was torn up again because, for my whole military career, a lot of things centered around me. I'll say me, me, me, because I have to go on deployment, I have to go on detachment. I have to be on watch at the expense of the family. It was one of the reasons I retired, so I could be there for them and not be away as much.

And now I had to leave again. I felt horrible, guilty, and like I had let the boys and Lisa down.

So the boys came home, and I apologized. "I'm so sorry, I gotta leave. I have to do this air show."

" Dad, we want to go to the air show with you," the boys said.

"You want to go to the air show?" I asked.

They said, "Dad, we've never seen you fly in an air show that we can remember. Of course, we want to go."

And I was really kind of blown away by that. But when I thought about it, they were right. I mean, I saw them watch me fly. But they were three and one, four and two, five and three at the time, little kids. They've seen pictures of me in shows but didn't remember being there and certainly didn't really understand what I did.

So then it changed, and we bought plane tickets. They flew into Phoenix, and the family drove down to Yuma together. It was really great on two fronts. The boys got to see me fly, which they said was motivating for them. And it's cool for them to see.

But even better was that as I landed after the first show and went over to see Lisa and the boys, their reaction was priceless.

"Oh, yeah, this is so cool. It's so great," they said.

Then Lisa said, "Oh my god, I had no idea air shows could be fun. Every time I went to an air show, the boys were in strollers. They were crying. It's loud. It was in the afternoon when they would normally be taking naps. It was a total nightmare every single time."

Her association with airshows was childcare and work. "This time," she said, "I had a great time. I drank a beer and watched you fly. It was awesome."

Not only was this a great move and a great community for me, but it was good for my family, too.

Things were going really well. Then came 2020.

26

POST PANDEMIC PATRIOTS

We did our last air show in late 2019, but then 2020 happened. All Air Shows and public events really stopped in March. One of the hard parts was missing my Patriot Team while we dealt with COVID.

For me, the camaraderie that came from my involvement in the team was really something special. All the guys on the team are just fantastic, exceptionally talented individuals.

When the Patriots came back together after the pandemic, things had changed, but some things stayed the same.

The Blue Angels practice or fly six days a week. After the pandemic, the Patriots had not flown together, even to practice, for 19 months. So there was some angst and some nervousness about our first time out. Since it costs money in the civilian world to pay for gas, not tax dollars, we only had two more practices scheduled before the season would start.

"Let's do two practices, just for comfort and confidence," we decided. "We'll clean a few things up. And then we'll go do the show."

So we did one more practice. There is nothing less dynamic in what the Patriots do than what the Blue Angels do. But the skill set and the experience of the team really allowed us to come back together and get back up to speed quickly.

That team dynamic puts us ahead of the game. And we don't change members every three years. It's the same pilots working together over and over again. Lisa calls it, "the air show, Masters' division."

A funny story about that first practice: as I said, it had been nineteen months, and we were exceptionally thorough as we walked through the show routine and the plan. We talked about all the concerns and the contingencies and the safety issues and what would happen if something went wrong.

Then it was time to go fly. The hardest thing we do is the six-plane loop, and it's right at the beginning of the show. In this practice, we did some warm-up stuff to get comfortable and regain the muscle memory of flying.

When I say a bunch, I mean, six turns, just a few quick maneuvers, then it's time for the loop. We went into it, and all six of us are looping, but it's not a Delta loop. It's a little looser than that.

But hey, it was a warm-up, and as the practice went on our flying got really good. We felt like we were right back at it.

When we landed, Bordz, the guy who was in my back seat the first time I flew with the team, came up and said, "Hey, Intake, man, I'm so sorry about that loop. I fell out. I just want to apologize."

"Bordz," I said. "What on Earth makes you think that I was in it? Don't worry about it."

It was a really cool and funny moment that showed our commitment to the team and being as good as possible, but that we were also human and made mistakes just like anyone else.

There are a lot of great things about the team. You know, both boys have gotten to fly with me. Nick got to ride through a full practice demonstration. Wyatt got to ride along for part of one. I asked Lisa if she ever wanted to fly.

"No," she said. "Because if we crashed, both of us would pass away.

"What? It's way safer than that, honey. It's probably more dangerous to drive in L.A. traffic."

"No, I don't want to risk flying with you," she said.

I completely understood. She is the more practical, pragmatic one. I am the one with the huge risk window, and it really creates a great balance in our relationship.

Besides both boys, my dad got to fly in a jet with me, which was a fantastic life experience. And so that's just kind of a perk of being on the team, but it's nothing compared to just the friendship and the camaraderie and the joy.

The Patriots also have a foundation that raises a lot of money for STEM education. I get to go speak to the kids in STEM programs that are the recipients of the funding raised at the Patriot Jet Gala. It's a really great organization and a fantastic addition to what I do with the Blue Angels Foundation.

The Patriot team members are also very familial. The men and women that are involved really care for each other, which is such a fantastic thing to experience.

I plan to keep doing this as long as they will let me and I am able. As of right now, I am the youngest guy on the team. I am sure the team will change over time, and I might be the last guy standing from this iteration. But I know a lot of former Blues that would jump at the chance to fly with us if we needed a replacement. I truly can't share with you how life-altering it was for me to join this organization, and such an honor to be asked to be part of it. The people that I've met and the friends that I've made, and the things that I've done helped fill the void left inside me when I retired from the military.

And Randy and I fly really well together. We both have similar risk tolerances. We're both passionate about it. It's interesting that if there's something going on and I have to choose between the Patriots and another event, I'm committed to that team, and I'm going to do the Patriot event.

It often takes a tremendous effort to drive to Denver, get on a plane, fly out there, and get picked up in another plane. The logistics of just getting to the Patriot hangar from Colorado is extreme.

When you explain it like that to people, they often say, "Oh, yeah, that's a lot of work." But none of it's work. I love going out there, spending time with the team. I'm the happiest and most content when I am flying.

My passion for flying is as much related to the adrenaline rush as anything. People often ask, "When you fly jets, what do you do now for fun?"

"Anything that creates adrenaline in my body" is my typical answer.

I can get my thrills in a side-by-side, on a motorcycle, or just getting out there and doing off-road stuff. The jets happen to have the same effect but are about ten times better than all of those.

I thank Randy profusely all the time, and he knows that I'm fully committed, which is why when opportunities come up, he trusts me to do things right and be all in, which is what it takes.

It's what many things in my life have taken, and the Patriots became just another part of the good fortune that comes from saying yes to opportunities. Those opportunities have literally been life-changing.

27

MAVERICK: THE CAST

Randy is an incredible entrepreneur. He put together an excellent cinematography company called Cinejet, along with Kevin "K2" Larosa. Essentially they were the first ones to mount 8K cameras on the L-39 trainers that we use. They built a new nose cone that allows the camera to film and the backseater to control the camera.

That's because it often takes a jet to film a jet, especially if they are simulating combat maneuvers. And if you need a platform that can be stationary but can also fly from place to place with the jets and get some really dynamic shots, a helicopter is what you need.

The company came together and bid on the aerial cinematography contract for Top Gun Maverick. And they got it.

And once they had the contract, they came up with this flight training regimen for all of the actors so they could learn more about flying and what jet pilots actually did when you are in an aircraft and essentially doing their job as a pilot.

They started with an aerobatic propeller aircraft to give them a sense of being in the air, and they were going to get in an L-39 before moving any further and acting in the F/A-18.

So in December 2018, Randy approached me because he knew I had trained pilots before.

"Hey, Intake, will you come down and help teach the actors about flying?"

Of course, I said yes.

Tom Cruise had his own training and flew exclusively with Randy. He got in the front seat a lot and is actually an accomplished pilot.

But we took up the rest of the actors and worked on anti-G strawline maneuvers and how that works in a real jet in real time. They learned all about G-induced loss of consciousness (GLOC). Basically, to make the film as authentic as Tom wanted it, they needed to know how to be fighter pilots.

To accomplish that, we trained them about where and how to look during various maneuvers, what one on one dog fighting looked like, and an overview of those skills. We did a lot of high-aspect passes, formation flying, and more.

We did all of this in the L-39 to essentially prepare them to transition to the F/A-18 for filming.

We did that for several days, and I spent a couple of weeks in California. That included Glen Powell, Monica

Barbaro, Jay Ellis, Lewis Pullman, Miles Teller, Greg Tarzan Davis, and Jack Schumacher.

It was a lot of fun. The actors were all excellent, receptive to instruction, and the crew was fantastic. But of course, I thought that was it.

It was a fun adventure, and it felt good to be teaching safety again, but I returned home, grateful for the opportunity and the fact that through saying "yes" to a unique opportunity, I had a chance to be involved in the sequel to the movie that had really inspired my career over three decades before.

But in July 2019, a call came, and I had a chance yet again to do something that would change my life once again.

TO HOLLYWOOD STUNT PILOT

In July 2019, Randy called me again. "Hey, Intake," he said. "They need a couple of pilots to film the final fight sequence. Can you come out for a couple of weeks?"

I went to Mike McCaskey, my boss at United. Hey, I have this incredible opportunity. I'll be gone for a couple of weeks. Can I do it?"

"Absolutely. This is a once-in-a-lifetime chance."

Once again, I said, "Yes." I could do that because of my relationship with United.

It came from my decision to say "yes" to running Fleet Week, "yes" to flying with the Patriot team, and "yes" to teaching pilots for the movie.

So I headed out to film the final fight scene with Randy. None of the actors, including Tom Cruise, were there. We did all of the flying.

It was just us, Kevin "K2" Larossa, and John Spanos, another great aerial cinematographer on the project.

From the point where Maverick and Rooster steal the F-14 to the recovery on the carrier, including all of the dog fight scenes, the flying was some of the most intense and dynamic things I have done.

Overall it took about two weeks. The first week was in the canyons. We'd get together every morning and do storyboard work and brief the safety factors. Then we would go fly the sequence.

It was ungodly intense. We were flying two or three times a day. John would be in a phenom jet, and he would do what was called pushing or pulling. He would either pull us through the canyon, leading us and filming us behind him, or he would push us through the canyon, in which case we would be in front of him.

They would want three angles of any given shot: pushing, pulling, and then stationary from a helicopter, which is where K2 came in.

I learned the three L's of movie direction: the right lens, the right light, in the right location. So we flew some of the sequences several times to ensure we had them right. We filmed for six days in a row in the canyons, and then we switched to filming over the water.

We did those sequences the same way: pushing, pulling, and with the helicopter. As you know by now, I have flown hundreds of combat hours, thousands of hours in F/A-18s, hundreds of shows with the Blues and the Patriots, and many hours in commercial aircraft.

The flying on Maverick is the most dynamic flying I have ever done.

Much of the time, the lead jet would be under a hundred feet, and the jet following would be even lower than that to present the right visual image to the camera. The canyon was tight, as you can see if you have seen the movie, and we had to constantly watch for obstacles while also staying in the frame for the cameras.

We got one shot flying toward the helicopter hovering overhead and then underneath it.

"That was great," Kevin radioed. "Can you do it again, only get a little closer?"

Closer? I thought. I was within feet of you, and now you want me to get closer?

But I did exactly what he asked.

I also remember flying over the ocean for one sequence, and a whale breached right in front of us.

"Did you see that, Intake?" Howler asked.

"See it? I almost hit it!" I told him.

There is a ton of trust between us and K2 and the other exceptional pilots. But we had to trust him, he had to trust us.

At that level of professional aviation, when I'm transitioning from demonstration pilot and combat pilot to stunt pilot, the trust required is even greater because you're doing stuff in airplanes that are unsafe by nature.

Yes, we brief it, we talk about it, we walk through it, even contingencies, and we talk about the safe recovery is something goes wrong. But at some point, you got to do it one way or the other to get the shot the director needs.

Effectively, I was a stunt pilot. I was not a Maverick stunt double, but we were "aircraft stunt doubles" who flew, in my mind, one of the most dynamic and powerful aviation sequences in film to date.

When it was all over, Howler and I went home. Then 2020 happened. So we waited, like many others who were anticipating the premier of *Top Gun: Maverick*.

We couldn't wait to see how our flying looked on the big screen.

29

THE RED CARPET

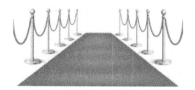

F inally, on May 21st, 2022, I went to the premiere of the movie. The first one I attended was out at Mirimar with the Marines because they had asked me to come out and talk to them about it. That was a benefit for the Gary Sinise Foundation.

It was my first time seeing the movie, and it all went so fast. I experienced it in a way that few do because when it came to that final sequence, I was looking for the scenes we had shot, trying to see our work. At the same time, I was really excited by the flight scenes overall.

But I also got to experience the movie in yet another dimension. Because as the movie started, I looked around. I could see the people in the crowd thinking, "Hey, this is really incredible."

But I knew then, in a way I hadn't in 1986 when the first

movie came out, what the deck felt like. It took me back to my time in the Navy. I could smell the jet fuel mixed with the salt air. I knew how slick the deck was and how it moved under your feet as you walked to your aircraft. I could feel the steam of the catapults and remembered the preparation and the feeling of the launch.

I knew what it was like to catch the wire and land, the deceleration the pilots would feel. I knew the closeness pilots developed with their crews.

I knew the sounds, the sights, and the feel of the events unfolding on the screen as if I were seeing it in four dimensions instead of three.

As you know by now, the club of pilots who have taken off and landed on an aircraft carrier is a small one, and few others would have felt the way I did.

More than anything else, I felt a sense of pride at not only the role I had played in this movie but in my career. And here was another film that would inspire the next generation of pilots.

I saw that premier, then immediately went to an event for the Blue Angels Foundation on the East Coast, and then came back for the cast and crew premiere in L.A., a private true red carpet event.

Lisa came with me for that one, and it was at Mann's Theater, which I think of as Mann's Chinese Theater. That was kind of surreal for me, too, because the grandfather of the first girl I dated at Pepperdine owned Mann's Chinese Theater and was a huge Hollywood movie guy.

My life had come full circle in many different ways.

By this time, I had seen the movie twice and was on the third time. I started to watch more closely.

Howler and I were sitting next to each other. It all happened so fast, and you have all of that energy in that fight scene. So when you watch, it's intense and fast. But that first few times, I didn't remember seeing us fly under the helicopter.

Finally, the fourth time that I saw the movie. Because I was super into the movie, I was able to sit back and watch the fight scene. You can see us fly under the helicopter well below 50 feet.

I realized, "Ah, it is there."

I was looking for it because it was so dynamic. Because there were some other things that we did, like fly vertically toward the helicopter that was hovering. The idea was you want to get the look down the intakes of the jet.

In order to do that, you fly up and get as close as you can to the helicopter and then bunt under it at the last minute.

It's one of the riskier things we did, and I wanted to see those things on the big screen.

Overall, Maverick, from the filming to the premier, from training the actors and spending time with them to the additional opportunities it brought, has been an incredible experience.

But probably the most important takeaway from all of it is that if I, a kid who watched Top Gun in a theater in 1986 just like many others did, can make all of this a reality, you can too. It's all about saying yes. Well, and a few other things as well.

But I've learned that I have experienced repeatable instances of excellence, and I want to share those experiences with you. Here's a little bit about what's next for Intake.

30

SAYING YES

I read an article once with Bill Gates and Warren Buffett. One of the mantras they had in common was to say "no." It didn't make any sense to me.

Instead, I say yes. If I don't know how I'm gonna say yes, I'll at least walk through the door. Once I get through the door, I can assess which direction I'm going to go.

Sometimes, but not often, I'll say no because I know that based on my 54 years of saying yes, the choice in front of me isn't the right thing to do.

When I said yes to shipping off my Blue Suit, I truly did not know about the action figure. And I didn't know about the poster. I did it because the Blue Angels needed help. And I was a Blue Angel.

Subsequently, these other things happened as a result of those decisions.

I got asked by United to run San Francisco Fleet Week

because I knew a lot about airshows. It's a lot of work. But that same year, I got to see the Patriots and bumped into the team.

That's when they said, Hey, we're looking for a guy. Are you interested? Again, I said, "Yes, I'm interested." I didn't know whether I was going to fly for them or not.

Then the Patriot jet team put in the contract for Top Gun. And when they said, "Hey, we need somebody to help train the actors. Will you do it?" I said yes.

These parts of my life are truly the result of saying yes and leaning into those opportunities. Each may pan out, they may not. But you don't know until you try.

So when people say, "Hey, how did you get to become a stunt pilot for Maverick?"

The answer is quite simple: because I said, "Yes." That's it. Yeah. Show up. Equally important is that I do the work when I'm there.

I'm currently working on my MBA, and people ask, "Why are you doing it? Why are you getting an MBA?"

The answer is that I always wanted one. And I don't know what will happen once I get it, but I'm pretty sure it's going to open more opportunities. And as a result, I've already met incredible people who are important to my future.

What I realized is that I have had a series of repeatable, excellent opportunities, and experiences that I have been able to capitalize on. My best friend, Bob, the same guy that I joined the service with when we were young, used to say,

God, you're the luckiest guy. We still joke about it. Because I truly am fortunate.

But that good fortune comes because I say yes. When I don't know something I need to know, I ask for help. I'm not afraid to fail. There were some incredible Navy pilots that wanted to apply to the Blue Angels and talked about applying, but they were so worried that they would not be selected that they didn't even try.

I went the other way. I'm going to give it everything. And if it doesn't work, like my application to NASA, then at least I know the answer.

Even a "no" is often nothing but good news.

But I also don't want to leave you with the impression that it all went smoothly all the time. You've seen through this text that my parents got divorced in the latter part of my high school career. I tried to balance my relationship with each of them independently of their relationship with each other.

My mom struggled. For the last several years of her life, my dad was always the bad guy" to her. There was a lot of animosity there.

My dad struggled financially when I was in college, and that was part of the reason I needed to work my way through school. He declared bankruptcy at one point, and the family home was foreclosed on.

As you'll remember, in the midst of my time with the Blue Angels, my mom passed away. I investigated the death of three friends during a short period of time and had to deal with each of those things without the luxury of time off just to sit and process.

Throughout my military career, there have been ups and downs. My first application to join the Blues resulted in failure. There were plenty of times when I failed.

But I learned from that failure and moved on. I asked for help when I needed it. And I continued to say "yes," while at the same time learning to say "no" to opportunities based on experience, not a hunch.

I failed applying for my dream job with United, perhaps the corporate job I was most qualified for there.

Closing that door and embracing other opportunities created the chances I have had to speak at large corporate events sharing not only my experiences but the blueprint they have created that nearly anyone can follow.

You and those around you, whether you are a CEO of a company or in middle management, or a leader of any group, can create a culture of excellence by implementing a few key elements I hope I've shared with you.

And if you have a dream, you can go after it, just like I did. Whatever your desires, you have to just keep saying yes, showing up, asking for help, and never fearing failure, and you, too, can get there.

From here, what's next?

31

WHAT'S NEXT?

T his has been the story of my life so far. It is far from complete. It's a story of a journey from watching a movie in a theater to being part of the sequel over three decades later.

It's the story of a career, or a series of careers if you will, each leading to more opportunities.

But it's far from over. This book is just the start, a beginning rather than an ending.

Because I'll keep saying yes.

The opportunity with Maverick led to another Hollywood opportunity. I'm learning more about business every day, and this will not be the last book I'll write. Because I want you to have the success I have had, and I think I have a unique message to share that can help you do just that.

I'll keep flying with the Patriots as long as I can, and I

hope to see you in the crowd at an airshow. I'd love to meet you and learn about your success.

I'll keep doing keynote speeches and workshops for companies and organizations, helping them achieve the culture of excellence I learned from my time in the military and my other life experiences. It's something nearly every company can replicate.

I'll also continue my work with the Blue Angels Foundation and increase my efforts to combat Veteran Suicide, which takes far too many good men and women from us every year. A portion of the proceeds from this book will go directly to them, and I'm proud to be a part of that organization and its mission.

Not only that, but I am sure other opportunities lie ahead. I don't know for sure what all of them will look like.

But I will make the commitment to you and to myself to keep saying yes, asking for help when I need it, and never fearing failure.

I hope you'll join me, going full throttle into life, knowing that what you do can change the world.

Until next time,

Scott "Intake" Kartvedt

August, 2023

ABOUT THE AUTHOR

Scott Kartvedt watched Top Gun in theaters and then went on to be a Navy pilot. He applied and was selected to be a Blue Angel, served during five combat deployments flying 91 combat missions, and accumulated over 6,300 flight hours, 658 carrier arrested landings on eleven aircraft carriers.

He went on to command VFA-83, an award-winning F/A18 Squadron and served as the Navy's first commanding officer of the only F-35C Stealth Strike Fighter Squadron in the US before retiring from the Navy and returning to civilian life.

Scott is currently a professional pilot and on the Board of Directors for the Blue Angel Foundation. He is an instructor and evaluator for United Airlines in Denver, Colorado, the number 5 pilot for the Patriot Jet Team, the only civilian jet demonstration team in North America, and was a stunt pilot in TOPGUN Maverick and was the aviation safety supervisor in Mission Impossible 8.

He lives in Colorado with his wife of 32 years, and his two sons are both naval aviators, following in their father's footsteps.

FOLLOW SCOTT KARTVEDT

Want to hire Scott to speak at your event? Find him on his website, https://scottkartvedt.com/

Follow him on social media here:

https://www.facebook.com/ScottKartvedt

https://twitter.com/ScottKartvedt

https://www.instagram.com/scottkartvedt/

A portion of the proceeds from this work goes directly to The Blue Angels Foundation for the prevention of Veteran Suicide. Want to be a part of this great organization and donate as well? Visit their website here:

https://blueangelsfoundation.org/

Stay tuned for more books coming soon from Scott Kartvedt!

Made in the USA
Las Vegas, NV
26 April 2024

89198997R00115